The Vision Casting Congregation

BY
DR. PHILLIP M. DAVIS

Orman Press
Lithonia, Georgia

THE
VISION CASTING
CONGREGATION

BY
DR. PHILLIP M. DAVIS

All Scriptures taken from The Holy Bible, King James Version.

Copyright © 1998 by Orman Press

ISBN 0-9652262-2-0

All rights reserved. No part of this publication may be reproduced, stored in a retrieval system, or transmitted in any form or by any means, electronic, mechanical, photocopying, recording, or otherwise, without the prior written permission of the copyright owner, except for brief quotations included in a review of the book.

Printed in the United States of America

WORDS OF ENCOURAGEMENT

"Dr. Phil Davis is smart and spiritual. He knows about church growth and he has grown a large and effective church. The Vision Casting Congregation *is our opportunity to learn from the man who can show other pastors and churches how to do it.*"

> Leith Anderson, pastor
> Wooddale Church—Eden Prairie, MN

"It was exciting to read of Phil Davis' vision and the blessings God has bestowed upon them as they have pursued God's vision for Nations Ford. I think the book is excellent....very good reading."

> Joey Johnson, pastor
> The House of the Lord—Akron, OH

"What is most significant is that seventy percent of this church growth is made up of new believers. They have started a mission church, and they financially support seven other churches."

> Joseph Stowell, president
> Moody Bible Institute—Chicago, IL

Table of Contents

Dedication/Acknowledgements 6

Foreword 7

Introduction 11

Chapter One
Strategic Plans Are the Foundation for a Vision 17

Chapter Two
Resources Flow Where Vision Exists 27

Chapter Three
The Vision Casting Congregation 35

Chapter Four
Establishing the Mission 43

CHAPTER FIVE
Leadership Development Is the Driving Force 49

CHAPTER SIX
Providing Choices to Reach People and Meet Needs 63

CHAPTER SEVEN
Building Temples of Obedience in Small Groups 71

CHAPTER EIGHT
Lay Ministries Create Synergy in the Body 89

CHAPTER NINE
Vision Casting a Little Further Down the Road 105

EPILOGUE
From the Heart of a Pastor 123

END NOTES 125

Dedication/Acknowledgements

This book is written in dedication to my Lord and Savior, Jesus Christ. He is the Source and the Resource for the Nations Ford Baptist Church, and anything that has happened for the good of the Kingdom of God has been by His grace and mercy.

I want to particularly express my gratitude and sincere appreciation to Susan Smith, who so patiently worked with me through this process.

Words could never express the depth of my love and appreciation for the encouragement and support from the Nations Ford Baptist Church family, and most of all, to my beautiful and gracious bride of twenty-three years, Cynthia, and our wonderful children, R.J., Bradley, and Ashley.

Thanks to each of you and to all those who have prayed for and with the Nations Ford Baptist Church.

The names are too numerous and the contributions are too great to begin any attempt at listing everyone, so please know that you are dearly loved and appreciated. Without you, there would be no "us." This is a team effort for a team vision. And the best is yet to come!

Foreword

While sitting in at an airport in England, en route to West Africa, I had the undistracted time to give attention to a manuscript that absolutely blessed my life. After being in the ministry for twenty-eight years, there are few authentic success stories like that of Dr. Phillip M. Davis and the Nations Ford Baptist Church of Charlotte, North Carolina.

I shall never forget being invited to preach the fall revival at this exciting church in October of 1993. This particular series of meetings left an indelible imprint in my mind because of the way I was led to formulate the teachings. The theme given to me was, "Seeking to Save the Family," and each night we addressed a different aspect of the family—male/female relationships, marriage, parenting, etc. In retrospect, I believe God was knitting together kindred hearts and minds. He allowed Pastor and Mrs. Davis, and my wife, Cheryl, and I to develop a bond of family unity that has grown through the years. Upon returning to Washington, D.C., Cheryl and I felt that we had found secure, lifetime friends in Phillip and Cynthia Davis.

Since our initial visit to Nations Ford, we have watched a strategic miracle take place in this "visionary congregation." Dr. Davis is a visionary leader, not unlike the Moses's and Nehemiah's of Scripture. Phil Davis lives, sleeps and breathes the visions and dreams that God implants in his heart. 'I will pour out my spirit upon all flesh; and your sons and your daughters shall prophesy, your old men shall dream dreams, your young men shall see visions" (Joel 2:28). God's Spirit upon Dr. Davis is evident in the way he has strategically practiced the principles outlined in this book.

Many people write and speak about vision and vision casting and church growth. In this book, the principles outlined transcend theory because Dr. Davis is a practitioner of what he believers. What you will read are not just concepts, they are real, practical strategies implemented at Nations Ford Baptist Church. What this congregation has become in just a few years is nothing short of a miracle orchestrated by God. While other churches are dying and trying to find a way to maintain members, this church has people standing in line to be a part of the Nations Ford experience. This after a humble beginning in Phillip and Cynthia Davis' living room with eleven people meeting for Bible study.

Dr. Davis and the Nations Ford congregation have been featured in *Leadership Today, Say Amen* and *Community Pride* magazines. In addition, Dr. Joseph Stowell of Moody Bible Institute writes, "Since 1988, as of this writing, (Nations Ford) has grown eleven to 1,500. What is most significant is that seventy percent of this church growth is made up of new believers. They have started a mission church, and they financially support seven other churches."

Dr. Davis and Nations Ford remind me of a principle I learned a few years ago. A careful study of the strategy of God reveals a pattern in how God shifted from the old paradigm, He never destroyed the old—He just brought forth a baby. Nations Ford Baptist Church was the new baby God brought forth to reach new converts in a visionary way.

Those who seek to move effectively in the twenty-first century and beyond will do well to embrace the proven tools and strategies of this visionary pastor and congregation. I can give personal witness to the end result of following these instructions. After serving as the director of computer services and membership at a church of several thousand members, I, too, gave birth to a "baby" in Washington, D.C., called Liberty Temple AME Zion Church just five years ago. With the encouragement and watchful eye of Dr. Davis and the assistance of the Nations Ford Baptist Church, the new baby (Liberty Temple) has grown to over 500 member and has seen over 2,000 salvation decisions on the streets of Washington, D.C. Using the concepts, principles and strategies presented in this book, Liberty has impacted the lives of thousands, because of the vision of one man…imparted to a congregation that became visionaries of great things. Pastor Davis is passionate about vision and those around "catch the vision."

I thank God for the friendship that we have and I praise God for using Nations Ford Baptist Church and its visionary pastor, to impart the passion for vision to many in the body of Christ.

> Rev. Charles Phillips, pastor
> Liberty Temple AME Zion Church

Introduction

God is glorified in the birth of a new church, especially when that new work becomes a spiritual explosion, experiencing exponential growth from the beginning. Between 1988 and 1997, Nations Ford Baptist Church grew from a core group of eleven to a high-energy congregation of 1450. How is such an expansion made possible? The church's ministry is transforming lives with the good news about Jesus Christ! The gospel is a powerful message capable of transforming every man, woman, boy and girl who desires to know God and His will for his or her life. People today are looking for answers. If they believe that followers of Jesus Christ can help them to be transformed, they will come. Why?

In our society, day-to-day reality is a multi-faceted experience of people, places, things, activities, and media coming from every direction. Several years ago, in a book entitled, *Future Shock,* theologian Harvey Cox described a world where we are called to intervene in the lives of people. He wrote: "Each person's life represents a point touched by dozens of systems and hundreds of people."[1]

Our lives are bombarded by change, running over with more information than we have time to assimilate. In such a world, "truth" has become a relative term, weakening its ability to be the sure foundation and guiding principle in many people's lives. How can the church make a profound impact for real truth in this kind of world—the kind of profound impact worthy only of the gospel of Jesus Christ? For human beings, making such an impact in our society may be impossible; but we know with God all things are possible. In the same way that the Bible is a book in which God reveals Himself to humanity, this book is about His spiritual explosion in Charlotte, North Carolina, creating a new church whose primary goal is to transform the life of every member so that each one can reach out and help save another.

Nations Ford Baptist Church is one of the fastest growing churches in the southeastern United States. Named for the busy thoroughfare on which it sits, during an nine-year period the church experienced phenomenal growth, and earned a reputation for excellence, innovation, and vision. Nations Ford is known for taking leadership training seriously and for doing it well. Since 1988, not only has the church family grown from a core group of eleven to an astounding 1450 members, but thirty-seven special ministries, all led by lay members, have also formed, and an average of 700–800 people attend the three Sunday worship services.

The Holy Spirit has drawn this family together with a bold witness that God's Word is the one truth holding the answers for today's world. The membership of Nations Ford is not ashamed of the gospel of Jesus Christ. It is a Bible-believing, Bible-teaching church with high expectations that its members will fully understand their vision, embrace their mission, and support the activities of the denomination. Nations Ford is a church for all people and all nations. It is a church with a God-sized vision, and endeavoring to keep the unity of the Spirit by avoiding extremes and embracing balance.

While the congregation is predominantly African American, there are also Anglo American, Hispanic, Asian, and charismatic and noncharismatic members also. The economic status of the membership is varied as well, including wealthy, middle-income, and low-income congregants. Educationally, there are members with postgraduate, graduate, four-year, two-year degrees, and some with no degrees. The church is comprised of dynamic, unique, paradigm shifters who reject being labeled or stereotyped—by the world, or the body of Christ as a whole. Black people within the congregation prefer to be called African American to acknowledge both their American culture and their African heritage. The common bond among the membership is balance, respect, and love for one another. A nontraditional church, Nations Ford has a teaching ministry with a special focus on family relationships, single adults, and economic development.

In the beginning, the core group of eleven made a commitment that we would be visionaries, always seeking

God's direction in growing the church through studying His Word, praying, fasting, and faith that He would complete the work He had begun in us. We asked God for vision, and He has given it liberally. In *20/20 Vision,* Dale Galloway describes vision as: "the ability or the God-given gift to see things which are not as becoming a reality."[2] Nations Ford is comprised of biblical visionaries having tremendous faith in God and in His ability to use them to grow a church. Hebrews 11:1 says, "Now faith is the substance of things hoped for, the evidence of things not seen." Each day at Nations Ford is bright with the hope that those things in the unseen will manifest and become real.

The success of the church is the result of this ongoing commitment to visualize a preferable future, to thank God in advance, and to count it done in the supernatural before it is realized in the natural. Visioning is a dynamic, ongoing process which never ends. The dreams of Nation Ford are set in motion by a process referred to as "vision casting." This means that with the wisdom and experience God gives today, believers within the congregation will choose their direction as a body of Christ with intentionality, and continuously project the picture of what will come to pass. Because this is done both individually and collectively, Nations Ford calls itself "the vision casting congregation."

I received the initial vision for Nations Ford in 1984, during my first pastorate at a small inner-city church in Charlotte. Realizing that the God-given vision would be manifested as a new church, my wife and I relied on Him to bring it to pass in due season. It is critical that visionary believers have patience and courage in allowing God to move in His time. We continued our work at the first pastorate for almost four years until it was time for the vision to become a reality at Nations Ford.

One core value of mine is "the law of the harvest," as described in *Principle-Centered Leadership* by Steven Covey, "The agricultural principles of preparing the soil, seeding, cultivating, watering, and weeding come before the harvest."[3] We can no more rush the harvest of a new work than a farmer can rush the harvest of a corn crop. I believe one reason God blessed our ministry at Nations Ford is because my wife, Cynthia, and I followed the law of the harvest during those four years—from the time I received the initial vision until the first worship service on January 3, 1988.

One of the most important things a minister starting a church must have is total and complete support from your spouse; not just platitudes such as, "I'm with you, baby." or "I'll pray for you." I'm talking about support in concrete ways. Without it, you're just setting yourself up for disaster—no matter how called you are. If you achieve the calling of the church while losing your spouse, you have done nothing, because your first calling is to your family.

My wife, Cynthia, has been my right hand through the years. She has helped me do whatever was necessary—right down to cleaning toilets, scrubbing pews, making bulletins, and cutting the grass. God certainly blessed me with a wife who has supported my call to ministry in every way. Without this kind of support, a minister shouldn't even make a move!

The first message at Nations Ford was "The Newness of Life," emphasizing our newness in Christ, and that as a church we, too, were new—with new ideas, new concepts, and new visions. Hard work, patience, and faith in Him are excellent virtues, and have produced fruit that will last. This is a story of a vision which became a reality beyond anything we could ever have asked or conceived. It is a story of encouragement for those who have vision, or who want to have it—clergy and laity alike.

Chapter one shares the importance of strategic plans in realizing a vision, while chapter two describes how resources flow where vision exists. In chapters three and four, the development and effective communication of vision and mission statements will be explored. Chapter five details how leadership development acts as a driving force for the vision and mission. Chapter six shares how offering choices in ministry grows the church, while chapter seven tells how small group experiences provide the most effective means of fellowship and discipleship. Chapter eight reveals how lay ministries synergize to produce eternal fruit. Chapter nine takes vision casting a little further on the journey. In the epilogue, I felt it necessary to offer a summary of what it all has meant to me as founding pastor.

I hope this story will encourage you to pursue your own God-given vision. Yours may be very different! Just follow the law of the harvest, and have faith in the Lord God that He which has begun a good work in you will complete it. From our humble beginnings, God has continued to show Himself mighty on our behalf. And we still believe the best is yet to come.

1

Strategic Plans
The Foundation for a Vision

> **VISION CASTING CONCEPTS**
>
> ✔ Vision for a new church is born in the heart of the founding pastor, and often results from dissatisfaction with the status quo.
>
> ✔ Strategic planning flows from the mental creation, or vision, that precedes the physical creation of a new church.
>
> ✔ Target a group for discipleship based on those who will be drawn by the personal characteristics of the church planter.
>
> ✔ Determine what approaches and programs will meet the needs of the target group.
>
> ✔ Choose a worship style that fits the target group.
>
> ✔ Determine an optimal location suited to attract the target group.
>
> ✔ Define basic expectations for membership.

A new vision, or paradigm shift, often results from dissatisfaction with the status quo, and precedes strategic planning. In 1984, I was not satisfied with being an African American pastor of an inner-city, African American church, relying on the help of suburban white churches to come in and do the work of the ministry. I asked myself, "What's happening here? Where are the mission projects of the African American churches?" My mother taught me that you don't make people into dependents—you raise them to stand on their own. I was not satisfied being a mission project for other people. I was raised to be a giver, a contributor. Generally, our membership and the people in the surrounding community had tremendous needs to which we needed to minister—making them less able to be contributors themselves. What could I do?

God gives believers the mind of Christ for a good reason—to be creative for Him! Steven Covey in *The Seven Habits of Highly Effective People,* defines the process well: "Creation is a two step process—mental, then physical. First, we must think and plan to create a vision, then the desired results will come."[1]

As my dissatisfaction grew, I prayed for direction and God began to give me a vision, as well as the beginnings of a strategic plan for action. The paradigm shift came when I realized that the answers to my concerns would come from the creation of a new church, even though my first pastorate had been successful in growing a new church to 175 members in five years. That small, inner city church had even won the Jewell Beall Church and

Community Ministries Award, recognizing us as the "Small Church of the Year" in the Southern Baptist Convention. The thought of leaving something successful to start all over again was certainly a paradigm shift not often embraced by the world.

I realized, however, that people primarily tend to worship along socio-economic lines, and that those who could contribute were not joining us because of language and geographic barriers. Middle class people generally don't come to the inner city for church membership, and their priorities in life are very different. One group talks about home ownership, and the other is concerned with, "How am I going to pay my rent?"

Great diversity exists in the African American community. We don't all think alike, hold the same values, or agree on politics. While we are not a homogeneous group, we share the strong bond of a common experience. Our common experience is that most of us have struggled to get where we are, or we have close relatives who have done so. In our diversity, the empathy and identity we share comes from the cumulative experience passed down through generations. Society and the media tend to stereotype people and put them in a box. If you can define and label a group, you have more control over their image in culture.

Each generation struggles to claim an identity in history. My grandfather's generation was "colored," and my mother's was "Negro." While I refer to myself as African American, I also realize that the key is knowing who I am. When you know who you are, no one can name you—you name yourself. My highest identity is that of "child of God," and God has shown Himself mighty in creating a new body whose members are first "children of God," and second, whatever identity they claim in the world.

COMPONENTS OF A STRATEGIC PLAN

The foundation for Nations Ford was laid in the strategic plans made by my wife and I during the four years between receiving the initial vision in 1984, and the first worship service in 1988. Our strategic plan included determining the target group for discipleship, how to meet this group's needs in a church, the style of worship this new family would embrace, the optimal location to draw this group, and basic expectations for membership. This kind of plan helped us decide what to do, and equally important, what not to do.

In *Strategies for Church Growth*, Peter Wagner comments on the need to focus on real priorities. He writes: "A great amount of God's resources go to waste because Christian leaders are majoring on the minors." Strategic plans increase efficiency, help measure effectiveness, permit midcourse corrections, unite a team, and make accountability natural.[2]

IDENTIFYING THE TARGET GROUP

African American churches in Charlotte were making a difference, but more was needed. God helped me see that we needed more training to help middle and upper middle class African Americans to think systematically and intentionally about serving and changing the world in the name of Jesus. The ministry of affluent African Americans, as well as others, could be more effective with a greater understanding of the proper motivation that underlies a true call to ministry. As I wrote down the ideas I was receiving from God, the vision and strategic plan for a new church began to form on paper.

The first step was to target middle and upper middle class African Americans with resources to contribute, and then teach them to be mission-minded individuals with godly motives for service, rather than guilt-driven or paternalistic motives which can perpetuate dependency in those on the receiving end. I believe intentionally identifying and drawing a specific population is crucial to the success of a new ministry. The purpose was not to exclude anyone, but to clearly identify the group of people we most wanted to reach. The corporate world knows this is good business, and used correctly, effective business practices can help build His kingdom. The goal would be to draw the target group, but all people would be welcome to join.

Meeting the Needs of the Target Group

Entrepreneurs realize that good business begins in identifying an unmet need, and finding a way to meet it. Truth exists in the old cliché, "Build a better mousetrap, and the world will beat a path to your door." People live to meet their own needs—an idea covered in-depth in chapter five. Since our daily struggle for existence is a quest for that which will meet our needs, it made sense to me that the design of a new church should take this important concept into consideration. When we have what people need, they will come to us. They will benefit, and the kingdom will succeed.

Cynthia and I took this line of thinking seriously. As representatives of the target group, we asked ourselves, "What do we look for in a church? What would meet our needs in a church?" We used ourselves as models in planning for reasons which Lyle Schaller outlines in his book, *44 Questions for Church Planters.* We felt fairly certain that the first several hundred members would most likely be people attracted by our personality, style, priorities, theological perspective, value system, vision, and world view as founding pastor and wife.[3] Since she and I both had successful backgrounds in the corporate world and in church planting, we planned to use our skills to draw others similar to ourselves to start the new church.

First, we decided the new church should be a teaching ministry where people would learn relevant, meaningful principles that could be applied in their lives immediately. In our post-modern world, many people are either completely ignorant about the Bible, or have very limited knowledge of its rich meaning. Many African American churches have great preachers or great choirs, but I've seen few with a great teaching ministry.

Second, we wanted activities and programs that facilitated significant relationships with others who share similar interests. I believe that life is a series of relationships, and that good relationships glorify God. We want to help people have the ultimate relationship with Jesus Christ, and have many other healthy relationships in abundance. Third, we wanted youth-oriented experiences for our children which would enable them to grow up in the church as disciples with skills transferable to adulthood.

CHOOSING A STYLE OF WORSHIP

Another component of the plan was choosing the style of worship most appropriate for the target group. We wanted to offer shorter worship services than most African American churches—which generally last around two hours. As part of this plan, we established two non-negotiables for worship: (1) only one offering; (2) no "dead" time in the service. We wanted an energetic, lively service that would keep the members on the edge of their seats with excitement. We wanted people to feel like they just had the best time of their lives in the presence of the Lord. Too much down time during a service causes the spiritual momentum to wane when it should be cresting. Also, we preferred two primary styles described in *Putting Your Best Foot Forward* by James Abrahamson. As a "reaching-up" church, we would be a praise-and-worship-centered congregation, where people come to sense the presence and glory of God. As a "reaching-down" church, we would emphasize the importance of knowing the Word of God. The entire service would build up to a powerful teaching sermon.[4]

Determining the Optimal Location

A critical part of our strategic plan would be the determination of the optimal location for drawing the target group into fellowship with a new church family. In *Twelve Keys to an Effective Church,* Kennon Callahan emphasizes the importance of open accessibility in choosing a location. Our target group would be busy with careers and family responsibilities, and we would need to be convenient to them. We considered visibility and accessibility because they can be such decisive factors in the success of a new church. It needed to be easy to reach, along a major traffic artery fed by residential and business areas, easily visible from the road on the high side of the property, with enough land to meet our needs for years to come.[5]

The Holy Spirit soon led us in a sweatless victory to find property that met this criteria in every way. Our location proved to be one of the most instrumental components in our rapid growth.

Basic Expectations for Membership

The last component in our strategic plan was to define basic expectations for membership. This would not be a church for spectators. Nations Ford would have high expectations for its members. We believed that members would rise to the level of involvement expected by the church. Lyle Schaller supports this thinking in *44 Ways to Increase Church Attendance,* "The New Testament makes it clear that Jesus projected extremely high expectations on all who chose to follow Him. The Christian faith is a high demand religion."[6]

In this church, our plan was that every believer would be a minister with God-given spiritual gifts to develop and use in ministry. We would be committed to excellence, meaning we would settle for nothing less than our personal best in everything we would do.

This was how we launched, casting the vision before ourselves and God—not doubting in our hearts that he would bring it forth in due season.

2

RESOURCES FLOW
Where Vision Exists

> ### VISION CASTING CONCEPTS
>
> ✔ Everything belongs to God, and He sends resources to those with a vision to do His will.
>
> ✔ A church planter must have an "abundance mentality," and think win/win in the body of Christ.
>
> ✔ Resources are human, material, and financial.
>
> ✔ Teach people the Word of God, involve them in the ministry, and they will give.

One of my strongest beliefs is that everything belongs to God, and that He will send His resources to those who have a vision to do His will. His resources are varied—human, material, financial, and I have never doubted that the resources to build Nations Ford would come. A church planter must be an entrepreneur, a risk taker, and one who thinks with an abundance mentality.

Abundance mentality, as Steven Covey tells us in *Principle Centered Leadership*, springs from internal security—not from external factors. It is a deeply held belief that enough natural and human resources exist to realize a vision, and that success for this vision doesn't mean others have to fail—just as others' success doesn't preclude my own.[1]

A win/win mentality is critically important for the body of Christ. Because my internal security rests in my relationship with the Lord, I believe I can do all things through Christ who strengthens me. I am never surprised by the way God chooses to send the resources, and I consider it a privilege to be a good steward of them. I had been a good steward during my first pastorate, and I trusted in Matthew 25:21, "Thou hast been faithful over a few things, I will make thee ruler over many things."

To be prosperous, we must meditate on His Word, act wisely, develop a God-sized vision, cultivate a network of winners, develop a strong work ethic, and be dedicated to finishing what we have started.

THE RESOURCE OF A LOCATION

The first major resource God blessed us with was an optimal location. Through the cooperative efforts of Dr. Bob Watson and Dr. Corbin Cooper of the Baptist State Convention of North Carolina, and Dr. S. Lawrence Childs of the local Mecklenburg Baptist Association, we were able to purchase a facility. For $250,000, we acquired a chapel and fellowship hall situated on six acres of land, located on Nations Ford Road just off Interstate-77, which connects to other interstates and has the highest volume of all the interstates in North Carolina.

Visible from the highway, we were easily accessible to the 1.5 million people living in the metropolitan Charlotte area. Many strong churches, new businesses, were already in the area and a coliseum building project had been proposed. We felt all these factors this would work to our advantage. The property was adjacent to seventy-five acres of undeveloped land that might be available to us in the future. This location was fantastic because of its accessibility, with high visibility on a road with high name recognition, which we used to name the church for easy identification by the public. This spot was so right, we would almost have to intentionally err in order to fail!

A good reputation and established track record of success in ministry come by following the law of the harvest, and are critical in drawing God's resources. The success of my first pastorate, on a small scale, made denominational support possible for the new church on the association level. The Baptist State Convention of

North Carolina contributed the first $50,000, and the Mecklenburg Baptist Association paid the mortgage in 1988, our first year. Our agreement was that Nations Ford would pay an ascending percentage of the mortgage until our assumption of 100 percent after five years. God blessed us richly as we were able to assume 100 percent of the mortgage in just three years!

Human Resources

God sends laborers to do the work of the ministry where a vision exists. Our initial group of eleven members grew to thirty-seven by the end of 1988. In this first group were three men who gave themselves completely to the new work, and went on to become the initial elders at Nations Ford. The first, Reginald Gabriel, was a computer systems analyst who had been a student of Islam. The second, Merv Snead, was a successful businessman. The third, Larry Morris, was an engineer. They, their wives, Cynthia and I, and all the others pooled our skills and resources in synergistic dedication to building the church. In this group was an abundance of talent for planning, coordination, outreach, teaching, preaching, and music. Like attracts like, and so it was that a talented group of believers shined a bright light which drew others of like mind and ability together. As pastor, I surrounded myself with a network of winners who got the job done.

We used every means available to publicize what we were doing via door-to-door outreach, public service announcements, word-of-mouth, newspaper stories, and through my radio show "Let's Talk About It" (see chapter nine). People like to join, serve, and give to a successful venture, and our membership grew quickly and steadily from the beginning. The talents and resources of 1450 members helped make Nations Ford the successful result of an ongoing, dynamic process of vision casting (see chapter three).

FINANCIAL RESOURCES

As I stated before, I'm never surprised by how God sends His resources! As we moved forward and held our first worship service, I was working a secular job to make ends meet while we grew the church. A gentleman I knew through another local Baptist church called to see how the new work was progressing. He was concerned that my time in the secular job lessened my ability to meet needs and develop the church. This was a wealthy businessman who had supported my first pastorate, even though he never attended there. He asked me for the monthly amount I needed to earn to support my family with a little left over for savings, so I told him. He then said, "Okay, I'll make sure you receive a monthly check for that amount for one year. Now go and do what God told you to do." With his help, I was able to immediately give my full attention to growing the church. Again, the vision had drawn a key resource. This gentleman has never been to Nations Ford—he just has the gift of giving. As a result, his east coast office supply company continues to grow twenty-five percent a year! His support was very instrumental to our success in the first year.

As our membership grew, giving increased naturally. If you teach people the Word of God, you don't have to worry about giving. Focus on their needs for spiritual growth, and they will give. Don't manipulate, don't push for money—one offering per service is enough. We teach our members the biblical basis for tithing and additional giving. Giving envelopes are included in the bulletin as people enter the worship service. Each envelope is printed with ten categories so that the members can designate how much of the gift is toward their tithe, additional offering, missions, benevolent fund, scholarship, etc. Our motto is "God loves a cheerful giver." Our cheerful givers have made it possible for our budget to grow to over a million dollars in a short period of time.

We believe biblical principles for giving apply to us collectively, as well as individually. For this reason, Nations Ford tithes as a church body, giving ten percent of our revenues for missions and helping other churches with needs. In return, God has opened the windows of heaven and poured out blessings so that we can be a blessing to others.

RESOURCES FOR PAID STAFF POSITIONS

A new church family with members as active contributors of resources became reality because of God's faithfulness in meeting needs where vision exists. Because so many of Nations Ford's members came with fully-developed talents and skills to use with their spiritual gifts, we were able to add paid staff positions to perform administrative duties because program functions were done by the lay members.

At the end of the first year, we were able to support a pastor and a part-time secretary. In the second year, the part-time secretary was converted to full time, and a full-time administrative assistant was also hired. In the third year, we added a fourth full-time administrative position. In just three years, we had taken over 100 percent of our mortgage payments, and had four full-time paid staff positions. Clearly, God was in control of the situation!

OTHER RESOURCES IN MINISTRY

Each ministry at Nations Ford currently creates its own budget prior to the beginning of the fiscal year, which is then modified and approved by a budget committee. All ministry leaders are expected to be good stewards, and expenses not covered in approved budgets are paid for by the members as gifts of love or by charging user fees for some special programs such as aerobics classes. Occasionally, throughout the year we have giving campaigns or encourage one time gifts for special projects or missions.

Vision, or seeing the picture of what we want to be doing in the future, is the key. For example, a vision for having a grant writing/development ministry began to develop in 1994. About six months into the visioning process, a talented man of God, who is also a professional grant writer and trainer, joined the church. Yes, God did it again!

We have an abundance mentality! Enough resources abound for all of us in the body of Christ to succeed beyond what we could ever ask or think. All we need is the courage to pray for God-given vision to guide our actions, and have faith in Him to bring it to pass.

3

The Vision Casting
Congregation

Vision Casting Concepts

✔ The vision statement must be concise, and must communicate the essential components of the destination you see for your church.

✔ The vision statement should be stated in broad strokes so that it will serve as a useful guide over time, through all the changes necessary for implementation of the vision.

✔ The components of the vision statement must have consistent definitions which are understood by the congregation.

✔ The vision statement must be seen, heard, and discussed frequently so that it has a high profile in the church family.

✔ To internalize the vision statement and have maximum investment in its manifestation, members must be taught and encouraged to see change as a given, and embrace it willingly.

God always has a remnant. When God breathes a church into existence, that remnant from the world is so powerful and bold that it cannot be denied. In our experience, the Lord took eleven people with vision and gave them the gift to move from one paradigm to another, while drawing together others of like mind.

The beginning is a fond memory—we were just doing our own thing! We began to grow immediately, and our first Visions Dinner was held in June 1988, when we were six months old. The purpose of the Visions Dinner was simple—a "state of the church address," and to cast a vision of where we were going. The twenty persons who attended looked back at what God had done, and looked forward to what He would do in the six months to come. All three of the initial elders and their wives were present that night, and it was an occasion for celebration and prayer. Since that time, annual Vision Dinners have been held in conjunction with the church anniversary and have been a cherished tradition in our church family.

Vision is the act of or power to anticipate that which will come to be. At Nations Ford, vision for ministry is a clear mental image of a preferable future imparted by God to His chosen servants, based on an accurate understanding of God, self, and circumstances. When members and staff are involved in creating this clear mental image, they become invested in it. At first, our vision was an ongoing conversation among ourselves about where we were going. We were serious, yet informal, regarding the vision until 1990, when we decided to hire a management consultant to help us crystallize the God-sized picture we saw in the future.

CREATING A FORMAL VISION STATEMENT

Our premise was that a growing church needs to have good sound business practices to be effective. We were interested in finding the very best consultants who could give us the philosophical and organizational things we needed. One person we used was very instrumental in helping us formalize our vision statement, and our mission statement (see chapter five). This consultant facilitated brainstorming among the staff, and then helped us state the vision's essential components in a concise form.

> **Nations Ford Vision Statement**
>
> *"Our vision is to become a regional full-service church, reaching people of all races, enhancing their quality of life by ministering to the whole man: spirit, soul, and body."*

This one sentence states a preferable future that many in the world, and some in the church, would find intimidating to implement. In *Dying for Change,* Leith Anderson says, "Christians of vision spend little time bemoaning the rough realities of our world and asking 'Why?' Instead, they look at the way things could be if the church were vital in prayer, devout in worship, informed in Scripture, aggressive in evangelism, close in fellowship, and zealous in missions—and they ask 'Why not?'"[1] Nations Ford embraced this philosophy, and made a commitment to be change agents for Jesus.

A pastor must be the primary visionary in any congregation. It is my job to see down the road before everyone else. When we began to grow, I saw that we would need a new building—it was crystal clear in my mind! The pastor must begin with the end in mind, and I am known for being a trailblazer. When I saw the building, it was my job to cast the vision before the staff and Officer's Advisory Board so they could then help me cast the vision before the congregation. All vision starts in prayer, and so we prayed together often, and at length. We didn't want to make a mistake! You can't take it back if you build the wrong building! When the staff and officers owned the vision, they were effective in casting it in the congregation, who received it with enthusiasm. With all of us in prayer, agreeing on the vision, it wasn't long before God made the way for us to realize the dream of enlarging our tent.

We also cast a vision of full-time paid staff members. The majority of African American churches may have paid administrative staff, but few have paid ministerial staff beyond the pastor. From the beginning of our existence, I prayed and immediately began casting into the first eleven members a vision for full-time staff in positions such as minister of education, minister of youth and children's programming.

If you try to cast a vision at the same time it needs to be manifested, it won't be as effective. Casting must begin very early so that people have time to own the vision, and catch up with where you are. With time to own, pray for, and prepare for a vision, little resistance occurs from those who will be impacted by the changes that come when the vision becomes reality. The successful casting of this vision for paid staff is the key reason that by 1997, Nations Ford had twenty-one employees, enabling us to be most effective in transforming lives.

REGIONAL CONSIDERATIONS

We concluded that 15,000 members would probably give us the resource base necessary to offer the full-service menu we saw in the vision. Reaching out to the entire metropolitan area of counties surrounding Charlotte would make it possible to draw 15,000 people with the expertise and financial resources to grow a large church. This would include at least one or two additional satellite churches that would eventually become independent. In our vision, we ourselves would be a large church, and we would be a mother church, starting new churches around the region.

FULL-SERVICE MENU

We envisioned ourselves as a "shopping center" church with a wide range of programs and services that would give our members and the community numerous choices for growth and support. A full-service menu would give us flexibility to meet needs in the most individualized way possible. Members and the community could access us selectively in the way most convenient and effective for them.

Reaching People of All Races

Our target group is African Americans; however, the God-sized vision includes all people. God directs us with His timing to bridge gaps so that people of all races will be brought together in exalting His name. We will not artificially force this into being, and we have faith in Him that He will do it because it is His will that we all be united in Christ.

Enhancing Quality of Life–Spirit, Soul, and Body

We are determined meet people at their point of need, in ways most convenient for them. All of our facilities are designed with this in mind. Before we had the resources, we envisioned a family life center, a 3500-seat worship center, and at least two services on Sunday, and a full education building, housing a kindergarten-twelfth grade Christian school and day care/after school programs. Our vision includes working for economic development in the community. We envisioned programs for singles, families, youth, discipleship training, physical fitness, and access for the community to use our facilities for workshops and conferences.

Vision Casting Is A Process

Vision casting is a tremendously challenging process. In the book, *Empowered Teams,* the authors share their views on the difficulties that visionary leaders face in leading people toward the vision. They write: "One of the biggest challenges leaders face today is translating their vision and mission into reality, and persuading people at all levels of the organization to pull together to achieve common goals."[2]

Once we had articulated our vision statement, our task became one of frequently and effectively putting it in front of the people so that they would become invested in bringing it into being. The vision statement has a high profile at Nations Ford in printed materials, banners, leadership circles, teaching plans, and messages from the pulpit. Everyone is expected to memorize it and be able to share it when needed.

One very key ingredient to effective internalization of and investment in the vision statement on the part of our members is the willingness to see change as a given and embrace it. A God-sized vision will require ongoing paradigm shifts as the process of manifestation takes place over time. Understanding and embracing change is emphasized at Nations Ford. Jesus knew ahead of time that His earthly ministry would only last three-and-a-half years, yet much of His teaching focuses on helping His disciples prepare themselves for the future. We desire to be change agents like Jesus as much as we desire to be change agents for Him. A vision casting congregation with a goal to do God's will cannot be denied—it will grow.

Growth produces change. Change produces challenges. Challenges make us healthy. Healthy things grow!

4

Establishing
The Mission

VISION CASTING CONCEPTS

✔ A mission statement describes what God is calling a church to do to realize its vision.

✔ The mission statement must concisely state the church's inner-most values, and be the solid expression of its vision.

✔ The components of the vision statement must have consistent definitions which are understood by the entire congregation.

✔ A mission statement should be true for the life of the church and serve as the bedrock upon which all ministries can be built and organized.

✔ The mission statement can be personalized and made real for members by creating a supporting mission action goal which describes the observable fruits that occur when the mission has been accomplished effectively in a disciple's life.

✔ The mission statement and the mission action goal must have a high profile in the church.

A vision statement paints a future picture of the church's ultimate destination with broad strokes. Once we know where we want to go, the question becomes "What will we do to get there?" Victor Frankl, Nazi concentration camp survivor and author of *Man's Search for Meaning*, says this about defining one's mission: "You don't invent your mission, you detect it."[1]

Each church body has a unique, God-given mission which can be detected through prayer, fasting, and guidance from the Holy Spirit. The management consultant who helped us form our vision statement also facilitated the detection of our mission. We wanted to identify the defining categories of ministry activities that God was calling us to perform to realize our vision of becoming a regional full-service church, reaching people of all races, enhancing their quality of life by ministering to the whole man: spirit, soul, and body.

IDENTIFYING OUR MISSION

Jesus gave His disciples specific instructions concerning what to do in the Great Commission. "Go, therefore, and make disciples of all nations, baptizing them in the name of the Father, and of the Son, and of the Holy Spirit, teaching them to observe all things that I have commanded you" (Matthew 28:19-20).

At Nations Ford, our primary purpose for existing is to be doers of the Great Commission by sowing knowledge, skill, and motivation into members' lives in order to reap mature disciples who would then be able to disciple others and build His kingdom.

We identified a mission with four major components, in line with Peter Drucker's thinking in *Managing the Non-Profit Organization:* "A mission statement must be operational, otherwise it is just good intentions. It has to focus on what the organization really tries to do, so that everybody in the organization can say, 'This is my contribution to the goal.'"[2]

> **Nations Ford Mission Statement**
>
> *1. Exalt the Savior   2. Equip the saints*
> *3. Evangelize the lost   4. Extend the love of Christ*

Our mission became a four-part operational statement. Our ministries will elevate Jesus Christ as Lord and Savior to the highest position in honor, power, glory, and character. We want to know Him personally, intimately, as a friend who sticks closer than a brother. We will praise and worship Him in Spirit and in truth. Our purpose is to do all within our control to eliminate barriers which might hinder a worshiper from encountering the exalted Savior.

Equip the Saints

To truly exalt Jesus Christ, and be ministers for Him, we must clearly understand who He is, what He has done, and what He is doing for us. This requires a thorough understanding of the entire Bible as God's revelation of

Himself. As a Bible-believing church, we will equip the saints to do the work of the ministry by educating them thoroughly about the Bible, and how applying biblical principles practically in everyday situations leads to victorious Christian living.

EVANGELIZE THE LOST

It isn't enough to save and serve ourselves. The first word of the Great Commission is "Go!" Our world is full of people who don't know Jesus, swept up in a society changing so rapidly that they have almost no time to react to the stressors they face. We will go to them, and preach the good news that victorious living and eternal life can be theirs when they give their hearts and minds to Jesus Christ so He can be Lord in their life. Our purpose is to motivate the entire congregation to "do the work of the evangelist," because we believe evangelism is not a series of events, but a lifestyle.

EXTEND THE LOVE OF CHRIST

As Christians, we are to love our neighbor as ourselves. If our neighbors are hungry, sick, in prison, poor, or needing clothes and shelter, it is our responsibility to love them as representatives of Jesus Christ. He came to serve rather than be served. He washed the feet of the disciples as a demonstration of what they needed to do after His departure. We will have ministries that extend His love, service, and concern for humanity. Our purpose is to have missions in the church, our community, our nation, and all over the world.

PERSONALIZING THE MISSION

We intentionally designed our mission statement for effective dissemination in the church family, and in the community. Beginning each component with the same letter lended itself to being attractively displayed in numerous ways as our "Four E's." It was then possible to create a logo to enhance our identity as a unique body of Christ. We chose a stylized cross on which could be placed the church initials N-F-B-C, and around which the four E's could be displayed. The mind of Christ helps us in creating witty inventions when we have a vision to do His will.

By 1995, the mission had evolved and expanded in two ways. In addition to being a four-point guide for creating annual, measurable ministry goals, it became the structure used for organizing the Officer's Advisory Board, church staff, and lay ministries into Ministry Management Teams. Prior to this arrangement, we were continually reorganizing our ministry structure around personalities. It took us four years to understand that relationships change, but the mission itself would never change. As a constant among many variables, it made sense to organize the church according to the mission components. Every individual's work at Nations Ford falls under Exalting, Equipping, Evangelizing, or Extending, and will be managed accordingly for maximum effectiveness.

The second evolution of the mission occurred after it was well established in the congregation, and had taken our thinking to a new level. We decided to personalize the mission statement with the creation of a supporting mission action goal which would describe the observable fruits that result when our mission has been effectively accomplished in a disciple's life.

> **Nations Ford Mission Action Goal**
>
> *"Transforming people's lives, with the help of the Holy Spirit, into mature disciples of Jesus Christ who will worship the Lord, express God's love to all people, and boldly witness to the lost."*

The mission action goal is the quintessential description of Nation Ford's purpose as a church. As with the vision statement, the mission statement and the mission action goal have very high profiles at Nations Ford. They are seen and heard constantly in all aspects of ministry. We are dedicated to communicating where we are going (the vision), what we will do to get there (the mission), and how doing the work of the ministry should impact each member's life (the mission action goal). Ongoing, redundant communication of these will maximize support and investment from the members and draw others who are looking for a church with a solid direction.

The Lord does things decently and in order, and so do we! The appropriateness of every plan for ministry is evaluated according to its compatibility with our vision, mission, and mission action goal.

5

Leadership Development
The Driving Force

VISION CASTING CONCEPTS

✔ People are motivated to join the church to meet their own needs, which can be predicted according to the characteristics of the target group.

✔ Mission-minded individuals capable of leadership are produced by discipling them at their point of need.

✔ Leaders should be drawn from the pool of committed, actively involved members in a new work.

✔ A strong team of paid staff should develop from within the church, from the pool of successful lay leaders, and form a nucleus holding all the forces in ministry together.

✔ The purpose of leadership training is to prepare potential leaders and their followers for success by teaching godly motivations, expectations, and accountability that will guide them effectively in ministry.

The story of Nations Ford unfolds as a system of ideas, rather than a linear or chronological description because our experience has been the simultaneous development of numerous ministry processes that interact and grow together. In this system, the process of leadership development has been the backbone of our success and the driving force in our ministry. Step one in creating this process was discerning what motivates people to join the church in order to determine the optimal leadership development method.

THE HIERARCHY OF NEEDS

We are all fearfully and wonderfully made according to His plan, which includes how individual motivation and behavior develop. People have a reason for everything they do, and in *Supervision: Concepts and Practices of Management*, the authors help to explain why: "People constantly are striving to attain something that has meaning to them in terms of their own particular needs, and in terms of how they see themselves and the world in which they exist. One of the most widely accepted theories of human behavior is that people are motivated and influenced by certain well-defined and more or less predictable needs."[1]

People are motivated to join the church to meet their own needs. These needs can be defined and understood in the form of a hierarchy. A well-known psychologist, A.H. Maslow, formulated the concept of a hierarchy of needs with five levels:

1. Biological (food, shelter, clothing)
2. Security (protection from danger)
3. Social belonging (being part of a group)
4. Self-respect (recognition, sense of accomplishment)
5. Self-realization (fulfillment of potential)

The first two basic needs are primary until they are met. Once they are met, needs in the higher levels develop.

Our target group of middle and upper middle income African Americans with resources to contribute would most likely have higher level needs. Lyle Schaller, in the March 1994 edition of the *Parish Paper*, tells us that society today is seeing a sharp increase in the number of adults on a self-identified search for meaning in life in general, and on a religious quest in particular. Our target group fit this description.

Expanding the Pastor's Capacity

A church's success is born in the heart of the pastor, but it cannot grow beyond the pastor's abilities unless that pastor expands his capacity by encouraging and equipping other people. My goal for the new work was to give it away to the members. This would be their church, where every believer is a minister, saved to serve.

I believe leadership training is the key to the growth and survival of any church, especially for Nations Ford. Our target group is motivated by a sense of ownership, caused by primary needs, such as having a sense of accomplishment and fulfilling personal potential, or self-actualization. Discipling members from their point of need meant intentionally creating multiple leadership positions from the beginning as one crucial way of meeting those needs. Members grow spiritually by doing the work of the ministry. For them, accomplishing the mission action goal occurs via on-the-job training.

Leadership in the African American Church

In predominantly African American churches, the pastor has the primary leadership role, rather than an advisory board, church council or committees. This style of leadership stems from our African heritage wherein the tribal chieftain was the leader of the people, surrounding himself with subordinates who would carry out his directives. These tribal chieftains went on to become leaders in the slaves camps in America. Interestingly, upon gaining their freedom, many became pastors, which made them the most powerful leaders in the African American community because they were supported by the church and not by the white power structure.

Historically, the African American pastor could speak his mind freely, and was under no obligation to local politicians or businessmen. The pivotal role of the pastor in predominantly African American churches makes it a little more difficult for Anglo Americans and some other cultures to join because they are not accustomed to direct, authoritative leadership from the pastor. This style of leadership tends to command lay leaders who believe in and support the vision, and doesn't leave a lot of room for those who don't.

PRINCIPLE-CENTERED LEADERSHIP

My emphasis on leadership development is based on principles that transcend racial and cultural barriers. I believe in principle-centered leadership, and my own ministry demonstrates that biblical and business principles can work together. While our style of leadership is influenced by our heritage, we don't focus on color. Rather, we focus on universal truths like vision, hard work, honesty, persistence, trustworthiness, knowledge of God's Word, and the leading of the Holy Spirit.

OPPORTUNITIES FOR LEADERSHIP

Allowing numerous opportunities for leadership proved effective in building a leadership development momentum that has snowballed over the years into the highly successful system in place today, which consistently grows new leaders in increasing numbers. By the end of 1988, we had grown to thirty-seven strongly-committed members active in ministry. Leaders revealed themselves by the nature of their membership.

Lyle Schaller, in *44 Questions for Church Planters,* gives good advice on identifying potential leaders from such a group. He writes: "If the vision is to create a high demand church, all volunteer leaders should be drawn from among those who participate in corporate worship at least twice weekly, are tithers, are committed participants in adult Bible study groups, and also carry other volunteer responsibilities."[2]

This description fit our core group of thirty-seven in 1988. They were all leaders in some way, and they wanted to know "What can I do? How can I serve?" I encouraged members to prayerfully seek God's will in developing plans for events and projects presented for my review. If an idea was compatible with our vision and mission, they were free to develop and implement it. This produced frequent short-term goal setting followed by achievement. This process of ascending achievements was a catalyst that increased confidence and risk taking as primary leaders emerged. I saw the vision and mission come to life when individuals began becoming leaders, able to minister to and disciple others. This was the dream come true—the reason we were born.

Effective ministry is dynamic, not static. I encouraged leaders to develop plans based on needs, and when the need was met, to disband the group that implemented the plan. That way, members were freed for the next challenge they needed in spiritually transforming their own lives in order to transform others with the power of the Holy Spirit.

THE NUCLEUS OF PAID STAFF LEADERS

An atom is held together by the powerful nucleus at the center of its universe. From the beginning, when we hired paid staff, it was natural to select from within. Dave Galloway, in *20/20 Vision,* gives a good reason for doing so: "If you want to build a strong staff that understands your vision, and will minister according to your style, then build your staff out of the people who are already being successful in doing the work of the ministry in your church."[3]

Involved, dependable members make successful leaders, and successful leaders make the most effective church staff. A strong staff team acts as a centering, grounding nucleus around which a church grows, and lay leaders develop. The nucleus of gifted staff leaders holds the powerful forces in a ministry together, and helps them to work together in glorifying God. Drawing staff leaders from within produces workers dedicated to a mission, not just a paycheck.

FROM PROJECTS TO ONGOING MINISTRIES

I was the first person in the staff leadership nucleus which, by 1991, had grown to four people. During that time, a number of lay leaders had evolved into various positions, leading specific ministries which served ongoing needs like preschool, Sunday School, choir, ushers, youth ministry, etc. By the end of 1991, we had approximately fifteen ongoing ministries led by lay leaders.

Six years later, we had approximately forty such ministries and twenty-one employees. This tremendous growth has occurred because we have successfully drawn eighty-five percent of our 1450 members from our target group, and we have grown the church in a manner that meets their primary needs. I have been and will remain open to new proposals for ministries that fit within our vision and mission.

The abundance of choices in leadership roles are available to meet the members' high level of need for a sense of accomplishment and fulfillment of their potential in spiritual transformation. Nations Ford members yearn for meaning in life, and transformational leadership builds on man's need for meaning.[4]

More lay leaders can develop when good members are able to choose to assume a leadership role in an area of ministry that best suits their gifts and talents. Self-realized leaders able to fully develop their potentials are vibrant and excited about being a change agent in transforming lives and meeting needs. They don't ask "Why?" Leadership who feel empowered ask, "Why not? Why not us? Why not now?"

Training Identifies/Equips Leaders at all Levels

I believe in training as many members as possible in the motivations, requirements, and expectations for godly leaders who exemplify Christ and build His kingdom. Some people who are trained may not become leaders, but anyone who has been trained for leadership will make a better follower because that persons understands what leaders are expected to accomplish.

Everyone is not designed to be a leader! Leadership is not just a position, leadership is also influence. It is being able to influence people to work for and reach mutually agreed upon goals. It is moving people from where they are, to where they ought to be.

Nations Ford has a continuum of training for all leaders. This continuum has developed over time, and will continue to evolve for the life of the church. All training is biblically based, multidisciplinary, and incorporates the best information available from church and secular arenas. Admittedly, I am not an expert in all areas, nor is any leader. Therefore, I believe that part of the pastor's job in creating a feeling of ownership among church leaders means keeping the leaders abreast of the needs and changes in our society by exposing them to great people, great places, great books, and great ideas.

Training prepares leaders for success. When leaders are trained they know what is expected of them. They know that they will be held accountable for their area of responsibility, and they are motivated to meet the challenge ahead. Training enables leaders to transition from one paradigm to another. In the words of Oliver Wendall Holmes: "Man's mind, once stretched by a new idea, never regains its original dimensions."[5]

Training for the Pastor

In addition to training leaders, is critical that a congregation support ongoing training for the pastor, such as budgeting for the purchase of training materials, for attending workshops and conferences, and for traveling to see great places and network with great people. The undershepherd of the flock has a high need for continued renewal so that a fresh word and innovative ideas can consistently flow in growing and managing the church.

STAFF LEADER TRAINING

Staff leaders at Nations Ford go through an employee orientation, and are given a manual clearly outlining their responsibilities. In addition to being active church members, they are to biblically, spiritually, and ethically represent our ministry in their public and personal life. Their lives must be an example of their relationship with God, and of their belief in the vision, mission, and mission action goal at Nations Ford.

Staff leaders are expected to be professional, empowering servants to the members and leaders, as well as effective team members with each other. Each must possess a willing spirit, an abundance mentality, and a commitment to excellence. Experienced staff are expected to mentor new arrivals. Attendance at weekly staff meetings and ongoing task-specific training in the community and elsewhere are encouraged, and extended staff retreats occur for ongoing skill development. Staff leaders also receive all the training designed for lay leaders as an added benefit.

OFFICER TRAINING SCHOOL

The Officer Training School equips godly persons who have been nominated through the recommendation process and who meet the requirements to assume roles of church leadership in the offices of elder and deacon, which make up the Officer's Advisory Board. The OAB assists the senior pastor in overall policy making and gives direction to the church as they are led by the Holy Spirit.

This school is a six-month instruction program in biblical truths, practical business knowledge, and interpersonal skills, with a goal to develop leadership and management qualities in the participants. The curriculum includes classroom lecture, on-the-job training, and group activities. Subjects covered include Church History, Major Doctrines of the Bible, Church Polity and Discipline; Church Growth Principles; Leadership Development; Human Resource Management; Decision Making Skills, and Roles and Responsibilities of Officers.

LAY LEADERSHIP TRAINING INSTITUTE

The Lay Leadership Training Institute discovers, develops, and expands the leadership and management skills of individuals selected as meeting the requirements for leadership and having the potential to be future ministry leaders. Selection is done by nominations from the ministry staff team, the elders, deacons, and myself as pastor. The Lay LTI is designed to be a source for consistent leadership development in filling vacancies over ongoing ministries.

The Lay LTI is a three-month training program with practical "hands on" application of leadership and management principles. The curriculum is designed to assist the participants in developing skills to effectively and efficiently manage a Nations Ford ministry team. Subjects include the Eight Principles of Leadership; The Laws of Leadership; The Mission, Vision, and Mission Action Goal of Nations Ford; The Four Central Areas of

Balance for Healthy Church Growth; and Major Doctrines of the Bible. A 3,000-word theme paper on "Major Doctrines of the Bible"' is required for successful completion, along with other book reports and group activities that foster team work. Each potential leader is individually approved at the end of training. The church does not guarantee a leadership position to everyone who completes the Lay LTI.

Once trained and approved for leadership, the Holy Spirit guides us in placing individuals over ministries that best suit their gifts and talents. The lay ministry leaders form our Leadership Council, which meets regularly as a whole, and by division according to the Ministry Management Team "E" under which it falls. An annual Leadership Renewal Retreat is a major part of their ongoing training. Outside training at church expense is encouraged for individual leaders, and is approved on a case-by-case basis.

Minister's Training Institute

The Minister's Training Institute prepares individuals who have expressed the assurance of God's calling on their lives for the five-fold ministry (based on Ephesians 4) in the role of pastor/teacher. This institute will produce persons who can plant and grow new satellite churches which will make up the Nations Ford Church Network. It will also be a source for the body in preparing men and women for other full-time, life-long church related ministry offices and vocations.

The requirements for this institute are rigorous, and training is open-ended, having no time limit. Candidates must have approval from the senior pastor, have their spouse's support, exhibit basic scriptural knowledge, and present a plan for the future development of their theological training. The process is a series of interviews, verbal and written examinations, readings, and reports. After successful completion of the entire individualized process, a candidate can become a licensed minister. To be ordained, ministers must serve a minimum of three years at Nations Ford or at one of its satellites.

QUEEN CITY BIBLE INSTITUTE

Nation Ford's God-sized vision includes developing leaders for the body of Christ as a whole. We want to glorify God in our entire region, and build His kingdom through our own church and others as well. The Queen City Bible Institute is a satellite campus of the Carolina University of Theology, located on the grounds of Nations Ford, and dedicated to equipping pastors, ministers, church leaders, and church members in our region to do the work of the ministry. In the QCBI, students can earn an accredited Bachelor of Biblical Studies degree, and a masters degree program is planned. Day and evening classes are offered and are open to all interested students. This is the crowning level of leadership development at the church.

This multitude of choices and opportunities in leadership development presents the comprehensive continuum we need to disciple members from their point of need, and gives them the opportunity to develop a sense of personal accomplishment, fulfillment of potential, and experience the ownership so important in their spiritual growth and maturation.

6

Providing Choices
To Reach People and Meet Needs

> ### Vision Casting Concepts
>
> ✔ Mission action goal accomplishment is enhanced by offering a variety of unique choices to reach more people for Christ and meet their needs.
>
> ✔ It is important to emphasize choices that meet the needs of your target group.
>
> ✔ Unique choices in ministry include the efficient use of current facilities, effective design of new facilities, godly use of technology, and convenient scheduling of church activities.

The year 1991 was pivotal in our evolution as a church family because we began to intentionally position ourselves to provide a menu of ministry choices to perform the mission which would take us to the vision. The intent to accomplish the mission action goal along the way was present from the beginning, long before we stated it formally in 1995. Since the God-sized vision of being a large church required growth, we needed to reach more people for Christ.

Choices Foster Growth

We believed the Holy Spirit would grow the church according to our ability to offer a menu of choices that would effectively meet the needs of our target group, because that is why they would become members of Nations Ford and remain there as active members. For our target group, choices included the efficient use of current facilities, the effective design of new facilities, the godly use of technology, and convenient scheduling of church activities. Chapters seven and eight will cover many other creative choices Nations Ford offers to meet needs.

In 1991, we created choices with what we had, and simultaneously began planning the construction of a new building in anticipation of steady growth. Our strategy was to build to grow, rather than waiting to grow to build. We knew that convenient scheduling was an important need for our target group to really be part of the church family. We also understood that having adequate facilities with sufficient space was needed to accommodate choices.

One important choice is the number of worship services offered each Sunday. We used outside consultation once again in deciding to have services at 8:30 a.m. and 11:00 a.m. to reach more people. Some resistance occurred in altering the traditional 11:00 a.m. service, but new paradigms ultimately create new traditions.

Offering two services caused us to grow, and by 1992, the 11:00 a.m. service was consistently filled to capacity. To avoid an overflow situation we added a third service, offering people three choices—8:00 a.m., 10:00 a.m., and 12:00 p.m. Meeting people's needs to attend church at different times was effective in drawing our target group into fellowship. When we went to three services, we were able to offer two sets of Sunday School classes at 8:30 a.m. and 10:00 a.m. With so many choices available, people could choose the services and classes they most enjoyed and which fit their schedule.

EFFICIENT USE OF CURRENT FACILITIES

In addition to meeting needs and offering choices, the tiered service/class schedule enabled us to maximize the use of our chapel building on Sunday by using it multiple times for numerous groups, rather than using it only one time for everybody. The chapel building measures 1700 square feet, and by the end of 1992, it was a busy place, housing three worship services and two tiers of Sunday School classes, Wednesday night classes, and our weekday AGAPE After school/Summer Fun Camp program for youth ages 6-13.

A Facility to Meet Needs

We soon realized we would need another building to accommodate the projected doubling of the membership every two to three years. Our vision included a worship center and an education building, but we decided to build our family life center first because of its potential to meet such a wide variety of needs—particularly the need for social belonging within our target group. As paradigm shifters, we weren't surprised by criticism from those who said it would stunt our growth because it was a gym, not a sanctuary. They saw a gym, but in our vision we saw a two-story 13,500 square-foot, multi-use building in which one part could serve as a gymnasium when needed. We believed that building the worship center first could cause the membership to fall into complacency regarding the other buildings in the vision.

The center took eighteen months to design, based on the vision God placed in my heart and upon input from the leaders and congregation, and local architects. It would be used for recreation, education, other purposes, and as a temporary worship center until the other facilities were completed. This building would meet needs for the current congregation and for those to come, while giving them an opportunity to strive for the realization of future plans.

God Provides Resources Where Vision Exists

Sunday worship service attendance averaged 400 during 1991-92. With such a short history, however, lending institutions were not a viable option in seeking the necessary building funds. Having a track record of ministry success in a large denomination like the Southern Baptist Convention again made it possible for God to send resources to realize our vision. We obtained a $625,000 loan through the Church Loan Division of the Home Mission Board (now the North American Mission Board). The nine-month construction project was completed during 1992. We implemented a "Together We Build" pledge campaign as part of the process to raise the additional funds needed and to get members involved.

Facilities Are Tools

The important thing to remember is that facilities are merely tools we use to reach people and meet needs, rather than monuments to human accomplishment. The facilities are the factories, and our members are the workers. In a growing church, there is a continuous flow of raw material to work with as people enter, are born again, and are discipled from their point of need. Unless members adopt this understanding concerning the use of building facilities, the buildings become an end in themselves.

Effective Design to Meet Needs

The family life center glorifies God in creatively and effectively meeting our needs as a rapidly growing church family. On the first floor, it has an aesthetically pleasing

5000-square foot "gymnatorium" which can be set up for worship services, recreation activities, conferences, banquets, or large meetings of any kind. Uniquely designed cloth "walls," functional indoor landscaping, cushioned folding chairs, and a movable platform stage with a plexiglass podium transformed an impressive basketball court into a lovely sanctuary in a matter of hours. It can be a banquet facility for up to 400 or a concert/theater hall for up to 600. It also contains a baptismal pool, shower/locker facilities, and a lobby where we distribute tapes and books, plus a brochure wall to disseminate ministry information to the members.

Upstairs, an indoor running track overlooks the gymnatorium, with a prayer room, a snack room, and multipurpose meeting rooms filling in the rest of the second floor. The size of several of these rooms can be increased or decreased with accordion walls that can be adjusted to fit the need. Every inch of space is used in this multipurpose, user-friendly building.

Meeting Needs Produces Growth

The family life center at Nations Ford has been an effective tool for meeting needs, and has been heavily used in the last few years. It is kept immaculately clean, and requires a full-time staff position just to schedule activities and supervise its use. Rather than stunting the church's growth, membership doubled during the four-year period after the center was opened in 1992. The facility has, in large part, helped to triple male membership at the church because of its open, non-threatening atmosphere. The environment is one that is easy for men to enter and enjoy.

Nations Ford is also meeting community needs by allowing the facility to be used by others for mentoring programs, adoption agency training sessions, homeowner association meetings, PTSA meetings, self-defense classes, and business workshops. The chapel and several other smaller facilities on the church property have uniquely designed uses to meet needs as well. Every square inch of every building is used as often as possible for a wide variety of purposes.

GODLY USE OF TECHNOLOGY

Nations Ford members have a high need for information and communication, and we believe in using the latest technology in meeting those needs. For example, in 1994, we installed a sophisticated voice mail system that dramatically increased the amount, and improved the quality of communication between the church and the members, and the community at large. A marquee with a strobing message in the family life center lobby runs an ongoing description of future church events. A lighted sign inside the worship area can flash the identification numbers of preschoolers to call the child's parents out of the service unobtrusively. We will continue to explore and implement new technologies that can improve our ability to disseminate information among the Nations Ford family.

The Holy Spirit is growing Nations Ford because the church has been effectively structured to provide a multitude of ministry choices which effectively disciple members from their point of need. When members' needs for social belonging, a sense of accomplishment, and fulfillment of their potential are met, they will be motivated to meet the needs of others less fortunate, and will become ministers for Jesus Christ to those who need Him.

7

BUILDING TEMPLES OF OBEDIENCE
In Small Groups

> ### VISION CASTING CONCEPTS
>
> ✔ People have a need to belong, but can only form a limited number of meaningful relationships in modern society.
>
> ✔ Meaningful relationships can be formed in the church, and are one of the most important catalysts of church growth.
>
> ✔ People will choose to form their relationships in church when the church meets their needs more effectively than the world.
>
> ✔ A comprehensive, ever-evolving learning continuum provided in small group experiences appropriate for the needs of men, women, boys, and girls will transform lives and accomplish the mission action goal.

Relationships and the Church

It is good for us to pose the question, "How can the church make an impact in our society, the kind of impact worthy only of the gospel of Jesus Christ?" The answer is that the church can offer what is missing in a fast-paced, technologically advanced society—meaningful relationships. While we may see advantages in living in this generation, Leith Anderson, in *Dying for Change,* describes a major disadvantage: "This generation has not been a good one for building strong relationships. In the midst of the huge population curve, many people live in isolation and anonymity."[1]

Anderson's statement reveals a great truth. People today need belonging and friendships as much as they ever have before—possibly more. The challenge for any person is that forming relationships of any kind requires a decision to do so, and a commitment of time and energy. In *Future Shock,* theologian Harvey Cox describes how we tend to form relationships: "Urban man must have more or less impersonal relationships with most of the people with whom he comes in contact precisely in order to choose certain friendships to nourish and cultivate. His capacity to know some of them better necessitates his minimizing the depth of his relationships with many others."[2]

Developing Relationships in Small Groups

People can choose their deep meaningful relationships from the workplace, the neighborhood, leisure organizations, or from many other organizations and groups in society. The church is also an option, and our desire is to be the place where members nourish and cultivate deep, meaningful relationships in small group experiences. At Nations Ford, many processes work together in transforming lives and making disciples.

We have discussed the importance of vision casting, defining the mission, creating a mission action goal, leadership development, and organizational structures that provide a wide variety of choices to meet needs. Each is indispensable, and all come together in a united effort to change lives and grow the church through small groups that foster healthy relationships which help meet the need for belonging so important in our society today.

Just like the human body, the church grows by cell division. I believe cells or groups within the church will enable us to grow into the 15,000-member congregation we envision. A megachurch of that size could be an impersonal place, but through a wide variety of smaller groups, it can provide intimate experiences where each person can be individually touched. If leadership development is the backbone of our ministry, then small group experiences are the heartbeat that bring us alive as a church family.

At Nations Ford, the most significant relationship is that between the individual and the Lord Jesus Christ. We believe one's relationship with Him deepens and matures through relationships with other believers who will walk with you, fellowship with you, share your joys, your sorrows, your pain, and other experiences of life, while encouraging, motivating, reproving, rebuking, and correcting you so that you can be conformed to the image of Christ, able to represent Him in the world.

Groups need to be small (eight to fifteen members) to be most effective. In *Individual Change Through Small Groups*, Paul Glasser gives us rationales for the effectiveness of small groups. He says: "The size of a group tends to affect members. Small groups tend towards higher rates of participation, greater individual involvement, greater consensus, and increased restraint among members. Relationships among people in small groups tend to be more intensive, and serious issues can be coped with more effectively."[3]

Our church is a kaleidoscope of groups continually changing and evolving in our quest to reach people for Christ and meet needs. Groups can be identified from every angle! To describe the abundance of group experiences at Nations Ford, a quote from J. Sidlow Baxter's *Explore the Book,* describing the depth of what happened on Calvary, is quite appropriate. He writes: "The different facets of the incomparable diamond are turned successively to the eye."[4]

As it is difficult to fully describe every view of a multifaceted diamond, it is also difficult to fully capture the plethora of group experiences at Nations Ford—it could easily be a book all its own! For my purposes here I will approach the subject in two sections. This chapter will address the group experiences available through what is typically considered Christian education. The next chapter will describe group experiences available in lay ministry.

Relationships that Grew the Church

In 1988, three groups were instrumental in growing the church. Wednesday night Bible study began to draw people truly interested in learning practical application of biblical principles. When people understood that they could apply the Word of God to their lives, they told their friends, and their friends told other friends, which brought steady growth in attendance on Wednesday nights. During the first two years, Bible study was like the old one-room schoolhouse—men, women, and school-age children together in one group, with me as the teacher. Wednesday night drew people who would then come back on Sunday for the worship service.

During this initial stage of growth, we also began Sunday School classes coordinated with excellence by one of the initial elders. These group experiences—Wednesday night Bible study, Sunday School, and Sunday worship service were friendly settings for those drawn to Nations Ford in the beginning. The friendships formed in these three groups cemented our identity as a new church family.

In *The Pastor's Church Growth Handbook #1*, Dr. Win Arn explains why personal bonding and relationship building among group members in church facilitates grow: "Friendships with others in the church is one of the most important keys in binding members to each other, and to the church. The stronger and more meaningful these relationships become, the more assured you can be that these people will become or continue as active

Christians in Sunday School and in church. There is a direct, positive correlation between the number of 'best friends' reported in church and Sunday School, and a person's own attendance and participation."[5]

This is not a new concept. In the early church, this was called the need for *koinonia,* or fellowship. Christian fellowship helps to disciple those involved. Programs don't change people—people change people. Fellowship means sharing and walking together as brothers and sisters—empathizing, sympathizing, praying, and learning what it means to grow up in Christ as a mature disciple. A large church must equip people to minister to each other. The vast majority of our members need to belong, to be part of a group, and our hope is that they will choose Nations Ford to meet this need. The world may have many ways for people to find belonging, but the church can do it most effectively because relationships grown in and centered around Jesus Christ are the healthiest and strongest.

A Learning Continuum Supports Growth

In the beginning years, the Bible study and Sunday School groups were the primary vehicles for church growth. They laid a foundation for the evolution of the comprehensive Christian education continuum available today at Nations Ford. This continuum is the most important program component for transforming lives and accomplishing our mission action goal because the array of group experiences offer something for every member as they grow in Christ. We want our members to grow, realizing that growth is a continual process. A teaching church must have an ever-evolving continuum for learning to be able to meet disciples' needs as they grow. People need to be able to advance in an upward spiral of growth or else they plateau in their spiritual development.

Two factors must be considered in the evolution of this kind of continuum. The first is that there are two groups to disciple—those who have recently been born again, and those who have been saved for some time. The second consideration is that the upward spiral of growth will be different for men, women, boys, and girls—regardless of when salvation occurred, because their needs are different.

New Christians and Seasoned Saints

New Christians are infants in Christ. They need to understand their new life, and be taken through sequential developmental stages of growth to become mature disciples. People who have been saved for some time may or may not have been in a teaching environment. If not, they can benefit from what we offer to new Christians. If they have been in a teaching church, our continuum offers challenging, advanced group experiences for those disciples who know the Word, but hunger to know it in its deepest, most profound sense.

Men, Women, Boys, and Girls

Adult men are the foundation upon which the family is built, and they comprise forty-two percent of our congregation. The Bible declares "If the foundations be destroyed, what shall the righteous do?" The foundations in the African American community have been bruised and beaten, but I don't believe we are destroyed. Men follow strong leaders, and they like the idea of fraternity or brotherhood. They need structure and absolutes. They want the truth, whether they like it or not. They are competitive, and love challenges, so we challenge them to learn and then live what they learn. We teach them biblical principles, and the results that follow when they are applied in life. Teachers must be committed and walk the talk before the men.

For the adult women at Nations Ford, one of their primary needs is to realize their secure identity in Christ, and experience His unconditional love. Women become strong and develop wisdom as they grow in the knowledge of the good news that Jesus revolutionized the role, and elevated the status of women. Women embrace the gospel with their whole heart, and many powerful women are attracted to Nations Ford in the quest of the deep calling the deep. They seek nurturing, supportive friendships in which they can give and also receive.

The primary need of children and youth is one they share with adults—the need for healthy relationships. Boys and girls need to see adults modeling an uncompromised, holy Christian lifestyle. They need genuine adult role models who speak their language, and show them the same degree of respect that is expected of them. When they find this genuineness in a teacher, they will embrace the beliefs and morals being taught. We challenge children and youth to learn the Bible with a fun, upbeat approach because we know young people accept challenges when presented well, along with love and high expectations.

A Unifying Theme of Joint Heirship

Despite all the different needs we have in the congregation, a unifying theme for the learning continuum is the benefit of joint heirship with Jesus Christ, incorporating a "Did you know...?" approach. We teach the uncompromised Word of God, emphasizing the conditions that precede His promises. At Nations Ford, Christianity is not a "religion"—it is a way of life. We look closely at "What would God say?" and "What would Jesus do?"

In our church, every believer is a minister! We declare this boldly because active members consistently demonstrate an applicable and growing knowledge of God's Word, and naturally evangelize those who cross their path. When you have something good, something that brings light and life, you want to share it, reach more people, and grow the church.

Building Temples of Obedience

We use "Building Temples of Obedience" as our slogan for our comprehensive learning continuum. First Corinthians 6:19 tells us that every believer is a temple because He dwells with us. In Matthew 7:24, Jesus tells us that whoever hears His words and does them is like a man who built his house on a rock. At Nations Ford, lives are transformed, and the mission action goal is accomplished as each individual's temple of obedience is built with Jesus as the Foundation and Cornerstone.

We want to help our members build or rebuild the altar of dedication to Christ in their hearts, because a transformed life will be completely yielded to Him. In the book of Ezra, the Remnant returns to rebuild the temple under a commission from Cyrus and God. Rebuilding the temple was a dedicated work of service and witness which restored those involved, and glorified God.

Biblical truths are always fresh! In another selection from *Explore the Book,* Baxter brings the Remnant's rebuilding of the temple to life for our time: "We are to erect a spiritual house of praise and witness to the Lord, in our own lives, in each local Christian church, in each community, and throughout all nations."[6]

OUR OWN SUNDAY SCHOOL CURRICULUM

God builds each temple individually, according to His will and in His time. Our task is to offer an eclectic array of learning opportunities in effectively designed groups to help our members grow in Christ, and to facilitate the healthy relationships that will grow the church. Toward this end, a communications ministry was formed in 1993 for the purpose of producing our own quarterly Sunday School materials for adult and youth classes. A small group itself, the ministry was comprised of gifted writers, artists, and support people who planned, wrote, created activities, illustrated, copied and assembled the materials that we felt confident would foster an individualized upward spiral of growth for each student. Books were printed, collated, and bound in time for distribution on the last Sunday before the next quarter.

In the first year, each quarter's curriculum was designed to effectively teach the biblical basis for the Four E's of the Nations Ford mission—Exalt the Savior, Equip the Saints, Evangelize the Lost, and Extend the Love of Christ. During the peak of production in 1995, we were we publishing 300 books every quarter, each edition taking four to six weeks to complete, with many hours of prayer in between.

This plan worked well for us for several years; however, in evaluating its effectiveness, we decided to disband the ministry for two reasons. First, creating and publishing our own materials was extremely labor intensive. Second, the expense of in-house printing was not cost effective. As a result, we returned to using the International Bible Lesson Series of Sunday School materials.

Even though we disbanded the ministry, we don't hesitate to experiment in ministry because we can learn what works, and what doesn't. In this case, we learned that individualized Sunday School curriculums were most effective when used to teach the mission of the church to the members. With this knowledge, other churches now contract with us to produce individualized Seed Sower's modules, one of which can help them design their own Sunday School curriculum, for a season, to effectively teach their mission to their congregation.

The remainder of this chapter is devoted to brief descriptions of many of the small groups in the Nations Ford Christian education continuum, which should help paint the big picture of the church's mission and ministry.

Preschool Ministry

This ministry offers Christian education tailored to meet the unique learning needs of every developmental stage in the preschooler population in building a strong spiritual foundation. Our ministry has grown to an average of 130 youngsters, up from the "charter" membership of approximately six children nine years ago. We serve three Sunday morning services, Wednesday night Bible study, and special services held throughout the year.

At the Sunday 8:00 a.m. and 10:00 a.m. worship services, we hold three classes of combined ages: Infants and Creepers, Toddlers and Twos, and Three to Fives. The 10:00 a.m. worship service is the busiest time, having the largest attendance. In order to meet this need, we hold six classes: Infants (birth–ten months), Creepers and Toddlers (eleven–twenty-three months), Two's, Three's, Four's, and Five's.

Our anchor teachers commit for one year to a particular age group. They prepare a weekly lesson plan, and are encouraged to assign a portion of the lesson to the adult and/or youth volunteer assistant for that week. This is another way to further involve non-anchor volunteers in the Christian development and training of our preschoolers, as well as provide informal internships for our ministry members.

New Members Ministry

The foundation scripture for this ministry is John 21:15-17 where Jesus says,"If you love me, feed my lambs...tend to my sheep...feed my sheep." This ministry is pivotal and sustaining in nature. Our goal is to begin the process of successful assimilation into the church family by providing the new member with knowledge and tools to learn about the church, and how to use their spiritual gifts in ministry.

New members' training comes in two parts. The initial training is eight weeks long, with members meeting for two hours each Sunday morning. Topics covered include church orientation, and introduction to basic doctrines such as salvation, prayer, praise, worship, and others. A spiritual gifts inventory is taken by each member to help identify strengths and areas of interest in ministry. The second phase of training consists of two discipleship training classes; one designed for the new Christian, and one designed for a more seasoned saint. Successful completion of the new members' classes is required for full membership, and for full participation in lay ministry activities.

Sunday Morning Small Group Ministry

As I mentioned earlier, the success of our Sunday School, or "Sunday Morning Small Group Ministry" (as it is now called) was vitally important to our rapid growth during the first few years. Before the family life center was built, we even had to rent space at local hotels to accommodate the large number of students attending classes!

Today, we have approximately 300 regular students in the equipping ministry, which is organized under the leadership of the minister of equipping and evangelism and has an adult education director, youth education director, and children's education director. The directors are responsible for effective use of classroom materials, securing and training qualified teachers for their own age groups, and working together to ensure a smooth transition when members age out of one group into another. We use the chapel building for the youth and children's groups, and classrooms in the family life center for the adults. Every room is packed on Sunday!

YOUTH AND CHILDREN'S MINISTRY

An officially organized ministry was formed in 1992 to meet the need of teaching God's Word to young people most effectively by grade level. This ministry has grown steadily along with the church, with many innovative programs that operate for a season until it is time to move on to the next level of program implementation. Youth and children are always changing as they grow, and we feel that a ministry designed for them must consistently present new and exciting programs to capture their interest and hold their attention. The most consistent thing about this ministry is that it is always changing!

When the family life center opened in 1992, we were able to give the entire chapel building to the youth and children's ministry to enhance their ownership in the church and foster more small group experiences exclusively designed for them in room design and visual appeal. At the beginning of 1995, we were able to hire a full-time youth and children's pastor to fully develop all aspects of this important ministry.

Grades one through six have their own worship services, Sunday School, and discipleship training classes. Older youth also have their own Sunday School and discipleship training classes, but attend worship services with their parents. Special activities like children's sleep overs, youth lock-ins, and Family Fun Nights occur throughout the year to promote their spiritual/emotional/social growth and development. The result is that children and youth are able to form healthy relationships with each other and their families while learning God's Word and having fun. Our hope is that young people will feel excited about getting to go to church rather than having to go!

DISCIPLESHIP TRAINING MINISTRY

Wednesday night Bible study has grown over the years from a general session into a general session plus additional specialized diploma classes up to fifteen members each, offered in thirteen-week cycles three times a year. This ministry is able to develop Individual Christian Education Plans (ICEP's) which offer the believer a systematic, sequential plan for growing as a disciple. Any member can request their own personalized ICEP, and a small user fee is charged for the classes to cover the costs to provide them. Examples of classes offered by registration are:

1. What You Need to Know Before You Say "I Do"—this course is designed for couples considering marriage or who want to be married at Nations Ford.
2. Beloved Unbeliever—the courses is targeted toward women with unsaved spouses.
3. Understanding the Blessing—the class is designed specifically for men.
4. Evangelism/Equipping Management and Team-Building Session—this course mandatory for all leaders in evangelism and equipping areas.
5. WiseCounsel—a course designed for those considering service in the following areas: Grace Groups, prayer, and counseling ministries.
6. Parenting by Grace—a course for those raising children or planning to in the future.

On average, 225 diplomas are awarded each year to students attending these classes. As a result of this and our overall ministry, for example, Nations Ford achieved the following rankings in the Baptist State Convention of North Carolina (BSCNC) and the Southern Baptist Convention (SBC) for one year alone:

	BSCNC	SBC
Overall—All Areas	#1	#18
Evangelism and Witnessing	#1	#5
Church Growth and Service	#1	#17

Thankfully, God has moved in the midst of this congregation, enabling the church to glorify Him with a reputation for excellent, effective ministry.

Grace Groups Ministry

Grace Groups are small home-based groups designed to offer support, love, and ongoing care to the church family, as well as outreach and church growth. Meeting weekly in people's homes creates a nurturing environment for sharing testimonies and solving problems. Grace Groups are strategically placed geographically in the community and offer a variety of different approaches to serious issues like loss of a loved one, physical, sexual, or emotional abuse, divorce, single parenting, chemical dependency, and a number of other topics. Grace Groups leaders are specially trained individuals called lay pastors who feed their sheep until the flock grows to ten or twelve members. Once a group reaches that size, it needs to restructure into two separate groups in order to protect the small group experience, and to reach more people.

Noon Time Power Hour

This weekly Bible study at noon on Tuesdays draws many people from the surrounding office parks who come during their lunch hour, and others who work at night or who happen to be available during the day. They come for praise, worship and to get a fresh Word for growth in their walk with Christ. Led by one of the Nations Ford ministers, it has been very a successful tool for drawing visitors to the church. The lasting relationships formed there can almost feel like another church within the church. It is a special group made up members and non-members, professionals and homemakers.

WORKSHOPS AND CONFERENCES

Over the years we have sponsored an increasing number of evangelistic and church growth conferences for our members and the public at-large. Some occur on weekdays, some in the evenings, and some on the weekends. Nations Ford sponsors an annual "Seed Sower's Conference." Participants from various parts of the city and state come to learn about growing a church in general sessions as well as small group concurrent workshops. We will continue to grow in this area because one of our most important goals is to help others reach maturity in Christ so that they can start new churches with their own God-given vision.

SOMETHING FOR EVERYONE

Christian education is a family affair at Nations Ford because small group experiences are offered for everyone! Men, women, boys, girls, seasoned saints, and new Christians alike find a place to belong, to develop meaningful relationships, to build their temple of obedience to Him, and to grow the church. It cannot be predicted what the small group structures of the future will be like, but for certain they will be designed to meet needs and transform the church family.

8

LAY MINISTRIES CREATE SYNERGY
In the Body

> **VISION CASTING CONCEPTS**
>
> ✔ True disciples produce fruit unto God, excellent fruit which lasts for eternity.
>
> ✔ Lay ministries are fruits born in the hearts of members who see a need and feel the call to meet it. Lay ministries will evolve when members are able to participate in creating them.
>
> ✔ Members actively involved in lay ministry groups have more opportunities to form meaningful relationships with others, and thus grow the church.
>
> ✔ Each ministry should develop vision and mission statements that are compatible with the vision and mission of the church, plus have a consistent organizational structure.
>
> ✔ Self-directed work teams expand the pastor's capacity, and give the members ownership of lay ministries.
>
> ✔ Lay ministries are synergistic when Jesus Christ forms the relationships between them in co-laboring.

The previous chapters have been devoted to the many concepts and processes responsible for the phenomenal rate of growth at Nations Ford. All of these principles and methodologies work simultaneously in building individual temples of obedience to Jesus Christ. In an effective teaching church, it must be remembered that knowing His Word is not enough—we must be doers and not hearers only. If we as disciples stuff ourselves on the Word without applying what we have learned and without producing fruit, we might become fat, lazy Christians.

In Romans 7:4, Paul outlines what true discipleship produces: "Wherefore, my brethren, ye also are become dead to the law by the body of Christ; that ye should be married to another, even to him who is raised from the dead, that we should bring forth fruit unto God."

MEETING THE NEED TO FULFILL POTENTIAL BY SERVING

Pastors walk a fine line balancing the importance of meeting needs versus expecting members to meet the needs of others as well as their own. For everything there is a season, and a time for every purpose under heaven. It may be the season to meet your need, or it may be the season for you to rise, pick up your mat and walk! Jesus said, "It is better to give than to receive," and I believe that the highest need among Nations Ford members for fulfilling their potential is met in serving God and other people. While our focus centers on developing church processes and programs that will meet a wide variety of members' needs, equal emphasis is placed on providing opportunities for members to work in ministry and serve others.

From the beginning, we cast the vision of a church where every believer is a minister saved to serve. Believers are to be obedient and sensitive to the Holy Spirit in using their spiritual gifts to do the work of the ministry. We desire to foster an open, creative atmosphere in which lay ministries could evolve naturally. Our hope is to produce godly fruit that will last because when Jesus Christ transforms a life, it is for all eternity.

LAY MINISTRIES ARE BORN IN THE CHURCH'S MEMBERS

The vision for Nations Ford was born in my heart, but the lay ministry groups have always been born in the hearts of members. Early on, I adopted the position that it was my job as pastor to grow the church and give it away to the members by allowing lay ministries to form when one or more members see a need and feel called to meet it. Members create a proposal and present it for pastoral review. If the proposal fits within Nations Ford's vision and mission, and it has been discerned that those involved are equipped to carry it out, as a pastor, my typical reply has been—"Go for it!"

Using this approach has facilitated the formation of an eclectic assortment of lay ministries—some serve for a season, and others remain active for long periods. Dissolving ministries that have served their purpose and forming new, relevant ministries has been, and will be, an ongoing method for creating opportunities for members to work in ministry.

THE LAW OF THE HARVEST MEETS NEEDS

When we serve God and others, we find our needs will be met because of the law of the harvest—you will reap what you sow. Anyone who wants to be great in the Kingdom must first be a servant because to be great is to be like Jesus, and He came to serve rather than be served. When the mission action goal is achieved and a life is transformed, that individual will be excited and eager to work in ministry.

CO-LABORING DEVELOPS MEANINGFUL RELATIONSHIPS

In 1997, Nations Ford had thirty-seven ongoing lay ministries, and other event-oriented ministries through which many members form meaningful relationships with others while doing the work of the ministry. In *44 Ways to Increase Church Attendance,* Lyle Schaller gives good reasons for creating numerous opportunities to serve in the church. He writes: "The larger the context used for program planning means more points of entry for newcomers, more places at which people can gain a sense of belonging, and more opportunities for people to meet and make friends."[1]

A large church can offer an almost unlimited number of opportunities to serve in small groups. Dale Galloway, in the December 1992 edition of *Ministry Advantage,* says this about the importance of building small groups: "Small group ministry is one of the most significant developments in the church scene today. Churches wanting to optimize their fruitfulness are realizing that they must develop small groups in some form."[2] At Nations Ford, we are committed to the small group concept for growth and fruitfulness!

LAY MINISTRY RELATIONSHIPS GROW THE CHURCH

One of the most critical factors contributing to our phenomenal growth over the last nine years is the fact that members can have small group experiences along two comprehensive continuums—Christian education groups and lay ministry groups. Whether it's time for an individual to feed or be fed, we have a group that is probably right for that person to find belonging, a sense of accomplishment, and fulfillment of personal potential. If not, that person's unmet needs will probably be identified in others as well, and before long, a new ministry may form to meet it!

This has been very effective in our church growth for two reasons. The first reason is keeping new members active in church. New members need to make six or seven new friends in the first six months after joining or they will likely become inactive. The second reason is that the youthfulness of our members make them prime candidates for service, eighty-eight percent being under the age of fifty. Approximately forty percent of our congregation are in the 26-40 age bracket—a very significant percentage. This is the fruitful time of young adulthood, and many in this group are drawn to Nations Ford because of its reputation for offering every member unique opportunities for ministry and service.

In *Dying for Change*, Leith Anderson describes the lay ministry potential for this group. He says: "These are the years of return, particularly as people have children. They also comprise the bulk of volunteer workers, particularly in the areas of outreach and nurture. They have children in the nursery and in Sunday School, so they are more likely to help out. They meet others their age through the school and sports activities of their children, which makes them effective in evangelism through relationship networks."[3]

An Organization Structure for Lay Ministries

Lay ministries are organized under the Four "E's" in our mission according to their dominant theme—Exalting, Equipping/Evangelizing, Extending, and an additional division for Operations/Administration. Following are the organizational groupings of our lay ministries into the four Ministry Management Teams:

Exalt the Savior
Director of Corporate Worship/Programs

Musicians	Creative Arts/Drama Ministry
Adult Choir	Sound Ministry
Male Chorus	Audio Tape Ministry
Single Choir	Video Tape Ministry
Praise Team	Radio Ministry
NFBC Singers	Pastor's Encouragement Ministry
Youth Choir	Hospitality
Commitment Counselors	Lord's Supper
Baptismal	Ushers/Greeters

Evangelize/Equip the Saints
Minister of Evangelism and Discipleship

Youth Ministry	Brotherhood
Children's Ministry	Victorious Women's Ministry
Preschool	Prison
Communications Ministry	Sunday Morning Small Groups
Adult New Members	Grace Groups
Youth New Members	Discipleship Training
Children New Members	Singles

Extend the Love of Christ
Director of Missions/Ministry

World Outreach	Food/Clothing Ministry
Recreation Ministry	Long Term Planning
Family Development	Nations Ford South
Child Development Center	Grant Writing Ministry
East Charlotte Fellowship	Parking Ministry
Volunteer Placement Coordinator	Prayer Warrior Ministry
Transportation Ministry	

Operations/Administration
Director of Operations

Office Management	Maintenance Helpers
Publicity	Facilities Upkeep
Newsletter Ministry	Security
Personnel Records	Financial Records
Pastoral Administrative Support	Membership Records
General Clerical	

These Ministry Management Teams are also subdivided into smaller teams under the supervision of additional church staff. Each ministry must have a vision statement, a mission statement, and a consistent organizational structure. For example, several ministries come under the umbrella of the counseling ministry.

Counseling Ministry Vision Statement

The vision of the Counseling Ministry is to become a full-service outreach ministry, ministering to the needs of all people. We will serve to minimize the occurrence of the "revolving door" syndrome by discipling those who have come forward for counseling via phone and mail. We will make referrals to other ministries. We will serve as an extension of the pastor by providing full coverage at each worship celebration, and during visits with other congregations.

Counseling Ministry Mission Statement

The mission of the counseling ministry is to evangelize by counseling individuals who come during the invitation for salvation, assurance of salvation, church membership, rededication, baptism, and commitment to church vocation.

Counseling Ministry Organizational Structure

The ministry leader reports to the director of corporate worship/programs, and is responsible for recruiting new members, training them to do the work of the ministry, and supervising the overall operation. The leader supervises six teams within the ministry, three that do direct counseling in face-to-face situations, and three telephone counseling teams—one each for children and youth, men, and women. Both sets of teams have their own organizational policies and procedures.

RECRUITING AND TRAINING LAY MINISTRY MEMBERS

Lay ministry leaders are trained to recruit members by first praying for the Lord to draw those who are called to serve in their area. A leader should be able to recognize persons who are being drawn, and offer an opportunity to join after all ministry personnel requirements have been met. Leaders also receive the names of members who have stated an interest in their ministry on the "Ministry of Helps" inquiry checklist given to new members, and readily available to all in the lobby of the family life center.

Leaders must train and disciple members to do the work of the ministry, then ordain or appoint them to a specific task according to their gifts and abilities. Leaders appoint members based on what they do well—not what they like to do. Leaders must model what they want others to do, and are to hold members accountable for completing their work. We encourage members to serve in one primary area at a time to enhance their effectiveness and prevent burn-out.

SELF-DIRECTED WORK TEAMS

To expand pastoral capacity and give the church away to the members in a way that they can truly experience ownership, lay ministries must operate as self-directed work teams, which are defined by Richard Wellins in *Empowered Teams* as: "an intact group responsible for a 'whole' work process or segment that delivers a product or service to an internal or external customer."[4]

Each lay ministry is responsible to work as a team in planning, acting, evaluating, and handling day-to-day problems as they develop and operate the ministry. Each ministry is a self-directed team, and is usually divided into smaller task-specific teams for greater effectiveness and retention of ministry members.

TASK-SPECIFIC TEAMS WITHIN THE TEAM

Creating task-specific teams within a larger self-directed team makes it possible for members to find a ministry opportunity in something they do well on a schedule that fits their lifestyle. It also allows them to work with others who share common interests. For example, in the criminal justice ministry, the overall team is divided into these smaller task-specific teams:

Criminal Justice Ministry Task-Specific Teams
- Bible study for inmates (males)
- Bible study for inmates (females)
- Visiting inmates (males)
- Visiting inmates (females)
- Visiting and serving families of inmates
- Letter-writing
- Baking cakes for prison staff
- Audio tape library

Members who join this ministry can select the task-specific team which best suits their gifts and availability. We can even find biblical examples of task-specific, self-directed work teams which come together as one larger team. Nehemiah knew what he was doing when he began to direct the large self-directed work team from the Remnant who rebuilt the wall around Jerusalem. Rebuilding the wall was a huge task! Nehemiah created forty-two different teams, charging each to rebuild that part of the wall which was nearest to where those members lived. This was the most convenient way to do it, and it gave the team members extra incentive to get the job done.

Many Nations Ford ministry members are content to specialize their service in task-specific teams, and we support this. However, we also encourage them to rotate through the various other task-specific teams within their own ministry, and in other ministries as well. This helps them to gain the more general knowledge and experience necessary for future ministry leadership.

A Healthy Church Is Like a Healthy Family

Many "best friends" form in these small groups during the course of co-laboring. Belonging, a sense of accomplishment, and fulfilling one's potential are all found here. Many people experience spiritual transformation as a result of the friendships and service found in the church. Healthy relationships form naturally when people work together to serve God and other people.

Does this mean that everything is perfect in our church family? No! Working together to feed the sheep can be a real challenge. When ten people are put together, they are going to have ten different personalities and cultural perspectives which can lead to problems. A healthy church will not be perfect, nor will they do everything right. Problems, challenges, mistakes, conflicts, disagreements, and frustration will surface. A healthy church, like a healthy family, will choose to solve these problems biblically, according to the Word of God, rather than reacting selfishly and emotionally.

Synergy in the Body

The crowning achievement, the highest goal in ministry at Nations Ford is "synergy in the body." Steven Covey gives us a good definition of "synergy" in his classic book, *The Seven Habits of Highly Effective People*: "Synergy means that the whole is greater than the sum of its parts. It means that the relationships which the parts have to each other is a part in and of itself. It is not only a part, but the most catalytic, the most empowering, the most unifying, and the most exciting part. Synergy unleashes the greatest powers within people. What results is almost miraculous. We create new alternatives—something that wasn't there before. It enables us to open new possibilities so that others can follow."[5]

Relationships exist between every principle, concept, process, plan, continuum, and group described thus far, because growing a church is the business of relationship building. Synergy is when two or more people, groups, teams, or ministries produce more together than the sum of what they could have produced separately. What do we produce in the church? What is our bottom-line for measuring effectiveness in ministry? Making disciples! It takes every principle, concept, process, plan, continuum, and group at Nations Ford working together synergistically to produce a disciple.

In the world, synergy is more difficult because it requires an abundance mentality, a win-win attitude, a willingness to seek to understand before being understood, and having a mutually agreed upon end in mind. In the natural, human beings tend towards self first, and others later. Synergy can be achieved, but it is more difficult to get there.

As believers, we are in the world but not of the world. We have been born again, and we are new creatures in Christ. For believers, synergy in the body will happen because we are united together in Him. When we truly allow the Holy Spirit to lead us, Jesus Christ is the relationship between the parts that make up the whole. We have been crucified with Christ, and we no longer live, but Christ lives in us. In Christ, we are able to work together synergistically, and God, through us, is able to transform lives and make disciples.

All of our talents, ideas, vision, and biblical knowledge put together cannot make one disciple of Jesus Christ. When we have truly submitted our lives to Him as Lord, and have built temples of obedience, His Spirit unleashes the greatest powers within us, and miracles happen. In modern society, it is a miracle each time someone gives his or her life to Jesus Christ and learns to walk by faith, not by sight. We don't make it happen on our own, individually or collectively. It is not by might, nor by power, but by His Spirit that we have become a synergistic, vision-casting congregation. Truly, all things work together for good for those who love Him and who are called according to His purpose.

Synergistic Ministry at Work

Let me give an illustration of this synergy in the body at Nations Ford. In late 1995, a twenty-seven-year-old woman who had been a member for years passed away suddenly after several years of serious illnesses. Many intercessory prayers had gone up for her during her trials, and she was more than a conqueror before us. She and her parents were core church members, having many strong, meaningful relationships with others in the congregation. Their faith, and the word of their testimony had been an inspiration to us all.

Her sudden passing was a shock, but experienced ministry members went into immediate action, covering all bases to meet the needs of this family, and the large number of extended family members who were making the sudden trip to Charlotte for the funeral. On the day of the funeral, every ministry needed was in full operation even though it was held on weekday, requiring most people to take a day off from work. Church staff, Victorious Women's Ministry, ushers, greeters, hospitality, choir, musicians, Brotherhood, parking, sound, preschool, and other ministries worked individually and collectively in synergistic, self-directed work teams requiring almost no direction from myself and my wife, Cynthia.

In the morning, the gymnatorium in the family life center was converted from a karate/aerobics class set-up the night before into a sanctuary for the homegoing service. When the service ended and the crowd left for the cemetery, workers immediately dismantled the sanctuary and assembled a banquet room able to feed the family of 150 upon their return from the grave site. Although our congregation was on the third day of a three-day prayer and fasting vigil, our members provided a full-course luncheon at their own expense, and served the crowd with cheerful attitudes. The entire event was upbeat—a celebration! When we have been equipped in the Word, absent from the body means to be present with the Lord, and that is cause to celebrate and give thanks!

When the family left hours later, everyone from all the ministries worked together to dismantle the banquet room, clean up the mess, and convert the gymnatorium into a basketball court for that night's practice with the 6-12 year-olds. Then it was time to ready the chapel next door for the evening's concluding service for our prayer and fasting vigil. I have been blessed to pastor such a synergistic congregation! In all of this, the members did the work of the ministry, freeing me to do my job as pastor in bringing a fresh Word to the congregation—praying for yokes to be broken and deliverance to occur in their lives.

God was glorified that day! When Jesus is the glue and oil in individual and collective ministry relationships, we synergize, and He is able to do new things in and with our lives. Synergy in the body is the only way we can accomplish the mission action goal and become transformed temples of obedience—mature disciples of Jesus Christ who worship the Lord, express love to all people, and boldly witness to the lost.

9

Vision Casting
A Little Further Down the Road

Vision Casting Concepts

✔ A God-sized vision will outlast you because His vision is from everlasting to everlasting.

✔ The church's mandate is to preach the entire counsel of God: spiritual and social redemption with justice, peace, and love.

✔ Only the church can guard the humanitarian interests of all people with the commitment of Christian love.

✔ The church can redeem the social order in the world, reach more people for Christ, and meet needs by building healthy community living for all people.

✔ In today's Information Society, knowledge is power, and the church has the most powerful knowledge of all—the gospel of Jesus Christ.

✔ The church can achieve its highest calling to preach the gospel to all people through the sophisticated use of media and technology.

A visionary pastor will always be looking a little further down the road than the congregation, and will cast the vision to them in stages as they are ready to embrace it. I see what lies around the bend, and it is a God-sized vision that will outlast me. The vision for Nations Ford goes far beyond simply being a great church to being a prepared bride for Christ. He will come again for us, and until then the church's mandate is to preach the entire counsel of God: spiritual and social redemption with justice, peace, and love.

Our vision to be a regional, full-service church grew out of a desire to create a church that would be the center of members' lives. Historically, the African American church was the place for meeting all needs, and it was the only institution totally owned and controlled by African Americans. In the past thirty years, many African American churches have lost this central position, but our God-sized vision calls us to restore the church as the hub of community living.

REFLECTIONS ON THE AFRICAN AMERICAN CHURCH

In *Economic Empowerment Through the Church*, Gregory Reed gives a concise history of the rise, decline, and need for restoration of full-service African American churches. He explains:

> "In slavery, the black church defied the hostilities that forbade it to be born, overcame the repression that sought to destroy it, and survived

to become the seed bed and the mother of the African American culture we cherish and struggle to preserve as our heritage. The black church knows the power of a holistic commitment by experience, for it was born out of a vast schedule of needs that a nation committed to slavery could not, or would not, address. Those needs were spiritual in the first instance, of course, but they were also physical, social, psychological, and economic. They were the same needs we recognize today as necessary to a reasonably dignified human existence. Since the black church was the only institution available to African Americans, it was by necessity all things to all people. The black churches gave spiritual refuge and assurance, but they also spawned the first black banks, burial societies, insurance companies, schools, and homes for the aged as support services to the spiritual needs of their people.

As America gradually opened its doors to include African Americans in selected benefits of citizenship, the black church gradually reduced (and sometimes forgot) the survival aspects of its ministry, and became focused almost exclusively on the life to come. We know now that such a determination was premature. Our secular institutions cannot be relied upon to guard with the commitment of Christian love the humanitarian interests of all the people. Only the church can do that."[1]

Redeeming the Social Order

God has moved mightily in the midst of Nations Ford, drawing together a powerful congregation of talented people who are well able to help us build a community as well as a church. The church's priority will always be the spiritual transformation of each member—but we are not content to stop there!

Once a people are spiritually redeemed, we need to redeem the social order in which they live to truly fulfill the vision of enhancing their quality of life—spirit, soul, and body. This can be done by becoming an economic stimulus in members' lives, and in the community.

People must be taught to apply biblical principles in dealing with the social problems that are literally crippling society—unemployment, underemployment, illiteracy, violence, and poverty. As stewards of that which belongs to Him, we, as His disciples, have an obligation to provide opportunities for people to learn business skills, apply them, and then launch out into the community to plant a seed of hope by starting their own business. When a disciple is able to apply biblical and business principles together, the synergistic outcome can lead to an expansion of community resources which can reach more people for Christ and meet needs. It is win-win thinking done with an abundance mentality to glorify God.

An unemployed member is raw material for the developing process. The Nations Ford approach is, "That's okay. Let's retool you. Let's learn some new skills. Get involved in the church! Practice! Do some things—be creative! Serve, lead, and refine your skills doing the work of the ministry—then go out and market yourself."

Lay ministry volunteers can acquire valuable training and experience in the church which makes them more marketable in the business world. For example, one very experienced ministry leader with a degree in religion was able to land a highly sought after social work position with a local agency, primarily based on her vast experience coordinating our counseling ministry and other projects in the church. On-the-job training within a large church is a valuable resource that comes to those who have a vision to fully develop their potential in accordance with His will.

COMMUNITY DEVELOPMENT AND THE CHURCH

I believe the church should promote entrepreneurship. We should promote business ownership, and help our members realize their highest potential in all they do. To achieve this goal, our church has been instrumental establishing the Nations Ford Community Development Corporation (NFCDC) to facilitate home and business ownership in our community.

In another selection from *Economic Empowerment Through the Church*, Reed declares the effectiveness of churches fostering the establishment of non-profit community development corporations. He writes:

> "As churches become more progressive in their efforts to meet the needs of both the mem-

bers of their church and the surrounding area, community development corporations have become the vehicle of choice for most church organizations to promote three goals: (1) economic development; (2) housing, and (3) job training."[2]

With a supporting organization like the NFCDC, the spiritual explosion at Nations Ford is poised for greater expansion as we work toward acquiring the seventy-five acres of undeveloped land adjacent to our property. The NFCDC has been offering homebuyers' workshops for several years, and one day I know that some of our members will be buying homes on that seventy-five acres.

In addition to our worship center and education building, our vision for this land and for the community includes new homes, renovated homes, a variety of shops, service organizations, medical offices, a senior center, a transitional living program to reintegrate prison inmates back into society, job training programs, as well as other unique projects to build a healthy church-centered community. The secular world has seen its limitations in redeeming the social order, and many outside the church are now ready to let the church step up and show what God can do about the serious problems we face today.

Building a healthy community to redeem the social order is a little further down the road, but I firmly believe it will come to be. I walk by faith and not by sight, relying on hope as described in Romans 8:24-25: "For we are saved by hope: but hope that is seen is not hope: for what a man seeth why doth he yet hope for? But if we hope for that we see not, then do we with patience wait for it."

BEING EQUALLY YOKED IN SOCIAL REDEMPTION

I am a patient man, willing to wait while God uses us to accomplish His will in His time. Although the Nation of Islam gets a lot of media attention for their successes in being an economic stimulus in the African American community, we have declined their offers for partnership in social redemption, much like Nehemiah separated his and the Remnant's affairs from Sanballat and Tobiah while they were rebuilding the wall around Jerusalem. In Nehemiah 2:20, he declares to them: "The God of heaven, He will prosper us; therefore we His servants will arise and build: But ye have no portion, nor right, nor memorial in Jerusalem."

We choose to be equally yoked in social redemption with those who are committed to the Lordship of Jesus Christ. We believe God will do it through us because the vision came from Him.

BUILDING HEALTHY CHURCH-CENTERED COMMUNITIES

A church-centered community will be a great benefit to all people—not just African Americans. People are people and have similar needs, no matter what color they are. The African American community faces serious issues, but they are an exaggerated reflection of society's problems in general. Nations Ford's vision is to reach people of all races, and we do. Although the membership is predominantly African American, there are members of other races who have their needs met, also.

THE CHURCH AND THE INFORMATION SOCIETY

In stepping up to the challenge of social redemption, the church must also be prepared to be a major player in the Information Society. Today, we often hear the phrase "knowledge is power" because information itself has become a key resource. For the first time in history, our economy is based on information resources which are renewable and self-generating. Science and technology have brought tremendous benefits to society, but they cannot meet humanity's most important need—to have a personal relationship with God. Only the church can do that.

We have the most powerful knowledge needed by every man, woman, boy, and girl—knowledge of God's revelation to us in the Bible, and through His son Jesus Christ. People hunger for truth that transcends the constantly changing nature of our world. People long for the knowledge of believers! This makes us powerful players on the information super highway, and in the political circles of social redemption.

If the church can be good for the entire community, and media facilitates church growth, then the successful use of media by the church is ultimately in the community's best interest. It is important for us to become sophisticated users of media to be most effective for being workers in the Great Commission.

SHARING THE GOSPEL ON THE INFORMATION HIGHWAY

Nations Ford is committed to spreading the gospel locally, regionally, nationally, and worldwide. Via the combined technologies of print media, telephone, television, and computers, a worldwide integrated information and communication system has developed which will fuel church growth as never before. In *Megatrends*, John Naisbitt describes the impact of such a communication system in our world: "This new integrated communication system will fuel the Information Society the way energy—electricity, oil, and nuclear power kept the Industrial Society humming, and the way natural power—wind, water, and brute force—sustained the agricultural society."[3]

We are blessed to live in this age, and it is upon the church to produce skilled leaders and entrepreneurs on the information super highway so we can bring more people out of darkness, and into the marvelous light. We are growing in this direction now, and look forward to what God will do through us in the future. Following are descriptions of various media, and our development in each.

RADIO—AN INTERESTING BEGINNING

Radio has been very instrumental in my ministry since 1981, before my first pastorate. My wife Cynthia was working full time, but I was going from job to job and we were struggling financially. We were down to just $100.00 at Thanksgiving and we decided to contribute to a new Christian radio Thanksgiving drive by giving $50.00, plus some clothing and canned goods. Even though that only left us $50.00 to live on, we trusted God to provide for our needs—and He did! God is good, all the time!

When I arrived at the radio station, the manager and I struck up a conversation. She said, "You know, you're interesting! I'd like for you to be on the radio. You could preach, teach the Bible, etc."

I replied, "First of all, I've never done it. Second, I don't have any money."

Her reply was, "Don't worry about your lack of experience—you can do this. You don't need any money, because I'll give you a half hour slot on Saturday mornings—do whatever you want with it. See you Saturday!"

You never know what God is going to do. All of a sudden, I was a preacher with a radio show called "Let's Talk About It."

My start in radio was quite serendipitous, but when God is in control, things happen in miraculous ways. That weekly show led to my first pastorate, where the vision for Nations Ford was born. Since that time, "Let's Talk About It" has become a core feature of Phillip Davis Ministries, the multi-faceted teaching ministry I share with Cynthia.

Over the years, "Let's Talk About It" evolved into a weekday program aired on four stations in North Carolina. The programs air during the prime drive times of 8:00–9:00 a.m., and 5:00–6:00 p.m., and have been effective in drawing visitors to Nations Ford. We regularly market church events before launching into a fifteen-minute selection from one of my teachings produced by the Nations Ford tape ministry. Listeners are given information about ordering and purchasing tapes, and tape series, at the conclusion of the broadcast.

AUDIO TAPE MINISTRY

In our quest to remove obstacles, the Nations Ford audio tape ministry regularly produces instant copies of the Sunday worship service messages from all three services for members who would like to take it home and hear it again. The Bible says, "Faith comes by hearing, and hearing by the Word of God." We encourage people to get the tapes because the message needs to be heard more than once in order to fully apply the principles in everyday life. Tapes are also convenient witnessing tools which make great gifts. We offer many wonderful tape series which are particularly helpful because of their ability to fully develop a theme for the listener.

Audio tapes are effective ministries that have transformed many lives. A member sent one of our tape series to her son in prison, and he accepted Christ from afar as a result of listening to them! He has since been released and baptized. He is an active member of our recreation ministry. People as far away as Texas have purchased advance copies of all Sunday worship messages for as long as one year! People purchase tapes with eagerness when they contain messages help them on their journey in life.

Newsletter Ministry

We have had newsletters in many forms over the years at Nations Ford, published by the church administrative staff, with help from the members. In the summer of 1995, an official ministry team was formed to take the newsletter to a higher level in appearance and content. The latest version is a professionally produced bi-monthly journal with an impressive, visually appealing design, and is loaded with interesting information. The ministry vision is to become the premier vehicle for communicating information about Nations Ford ministries and the Word of God, and to create publications that address the specific needs of its readers.

Books, Pamphlets, Study Guides, Etc.

We also see other kinds of print media doing the work of the ministry such as books, pamphlets, and study guides, as well as magazine and newspaper articles. This book, for example, is just the first of a series of books I will write during my life as a pastor/teacher. I have been inspired, and have learned great things about ministry and life from books. I hope to help others grow by making a significant contribution through books in the years to come.

We regularly submit articles to the newspaper, and have been quite successful in being featured, being mentioned in articles, and being quoted on community affairs. Even if an article is not printed, it will be added to a growing cumulative file on the church, which are used as we build our reputation in the region. I have had biblical essay columns in local magazines, and we have been featured often in the Metrolina Baptist Ministries newsletters. All of these avenues reach a different segment of the readers in our area, and help draw visitors to our church to find out about the spiritual explosion at 7410 Nations Ford Road.

Study guides, booklets, pamphlets, and brochures also help us provide the maximum number of opportunities to reach more people for Christ, and teach biblical principles that lead to victorious living. We are very busy evolving this ministry component because these kinds of printed materials work hand-in-hand to support other ministry projects and activities in spreading the gospel to all people.

Television

Television is a new venture for us at Nations Ford. Since 1993, we have produced a thirty-minute, monthly program called "Wisdom for Today," which airs on a local cable access channel. We are experimenting with television on cable access in order to develop excellent technical skills, and work out all of the bugs. The television ministry at Nations Ford is still in a stage of infancy with television, and we recognize that we will make mistakes along the way. We are committed to the process, however, and feel the long term benefits will be worth the present. Our vision includes broadcasting our worship services, and other syndicated programs both regionally and nationally on secular channels because most lost people don't watch the exclusively religious channels. Through television, we aim to evangelize the lost—not those who already know Jesus as Lord and Savior.

E-MAIL AND ONLINE SERVICES

Nations Ford will always be ready to embrace the latest technology when it can be used to advance the kingdom of God. E-mail and online services are two evangelistic methods we will be developing fully in the years to come. Small beginnings here already show great promise. In a recent e-mail conversation, I led a man to the Lord who has since been a visitor at Nations Ford.

God is sovereign, and He can do anything He wants—even using e-mail in bringing someone into a relationship with Him. We don't know exactly how computer networking will be used in our ministry, but we are sure that it will be a part of the big picture because of its ability to reach people for Christ and meet needs.

WORLD OUTREACH MINISTRY

As Nations Ford grows and expands, our God-sized vision does, too. We see spreading the gospel and redeeming the social order as encompassing the world! In the Great Commission (Matthew 28:19-20), Jesus instructed His disciples to *go* and teach *all nations* to observe His commandments, and we take this responsibility seriously. Jesus didn't ask us to evangelize all nations, He issued a mandate! The time has come for us, the Church, to mobilize ourselves for the cause of Christ, not only in our city, state, and nation, but around the world as well. To help accomplish this goal, a world outreach ministry was formed at Nations Ford in 1994 to develop a world missions strategy for the church, set long- and short-term goals for mission projects, and stimulate world missions giving.

In 1995, we began this work in earnest by sending out two teams on missions projects—one to the Mississippi Delta Valley, and the second to Nairobi, Kenya, for the purpose of spreading the gospel, building churches, renovating homes, and building relationships. These projects were funded by the church, the mission team members themselves, and a pledge campaign wherein each church member was able to personally contribute and support the mission teams in accomplishing their goals. Both projects were highly successful—over 100 people gave their lives to Christ as a result of the Holy Spirit working in and through us! We rejoiced in this victory—pausing only for a moment before moving forward with the vision.

Future plans include similar mission trips, as well as underwriting support for specific missionaries, workshops, seminars, missions festivals, and corporate prayer activities within the church. We think and act with an abundance mentality, trusting God for the resources to meet this tremendous challenge in reaching the world for Him.

Social Redeemers and Masters of Media

Redeeming the social order and mastering the sophisticated use of a continuum of media, from radio to e-mail, is a tremendous challenge with certain associated risks that must be embraced. In our Information Society, systems are obsolete soon after their creation, so our commitment in these areas is for the long run. We anticipate progress in peaks and valleys, successes as well as mistakes, and a process that will ultimately be an upward spiral of growth in the end. The philosopher Goethe also viewed progress in this way, expressing these words of wisdom: "Progress has not followed a straight, ascending line, but a spiral with rhythms of progress and retrogression, of evolution, and dissolution."[4]

A God-sized vision must be embraced with total trust and faith in Him that He will do it through us in His way, and in His time. Being effective social redeemers and masters of media are a little further down the road in our vision, but it isn't how you start that matters—it's how you finish!

A Time for Management and Learning to Wait

Following a period of extraordinary growth, Nations Ford entered a period of needing to manage all its gift and blessings and learning to wait for what will come. Growth has happened so quickly at Nations Ford that sometimes it becomes difficult for the congregation to wait for things! We must avoid thinking that everything needs to happen immediately! The church must allow God to move in His time, because His timing is always perfect. Our focus into the next century will be exercising good stewardship over all the resources with which God has blessed us.

NATIONS FORD—A 21ST CENTURY CHURCH

We have a tremendous testimony at Nations Ford! The vision born out of dissatisfaction with the status quo in 1984 has become a powerful and unique church family that glorifies God. He has been working through us, fearfully and wonderfully designing a new twenty-first century church. He has done a new thing in us by drawing resources so that we can offer choices to meet needs and transform lives.

He has taken us as the potter takes the clay, and has formed an internal structure of small group experiences that facilitate healthy relationships in Himself, so that our members' core group of healthy relationships will exist in the church family as opposed to in the world.

Our church family transcends time and place in the Information Society through radio, television, tapes, books, other printed materials, computer networking and world outreach. New kinds of healthy relationships will develop in the twenty-first century by the excellent, godly use of science and technology capable of reaching the entire world for Jesus Christ. Surely, we are coming near to the time of His return!

Relationships abound between individual members, between members and the church, between the church and the community, and between the church and the world. God is the One who breathes life, light, and love into these relationships, causing them to synergize in ministry, meet needs, and accomplish the mission action goal of the Great Commission—making disciples.

We consider it a privilege to serve Him as we help people along life's journey to go from victory to victory, and faith step to faith step, growing in grace and knowledge of Jesus Christ as Lord and Savior.

EPILOGUE
From the Heart of the Pastor

The story of Nations Ford Baptist Church is a part of me because the vision born in my heart comes out of who I am. There is nothing else in life I could do or would want to do. When the Lord saved me, I became aware that I didn't choose Him, but He chose me that I should go and bring forth much fruit—fruit that shall remain. This rhema from God was spoken into my heart in the late 1970's when I was desperate for guidance in ministry.

I needed to know that this Jesus thing was real, because I didn't want to waste my life on an illusion or a myth. Rhema from God showed me that I must launch out into the deep, and let down my net so that He can draw people unto Himself. Once I knew my calling, my course was set and nothing could change my mind. I can speak confidently, boldly, and with authority because I know that if everybody left me, I would still be doing the same thing and God would provide. It is His work, not mine. Therefore, my only responsibility is to be faithful in serving Him.

As a man of high expectations, I will never be satisfied with the status quo. I will always be the one looking for what lies ahead a little further down the road. I will always be a vision-caster for God. I never wanted to be average because that's either the best of the worst, or the worst of the best. Average is in the middle. It's being lukewarm, and anyone can do that. Being a vision caster requires me to push myself as well as others out of our comfort zones, and even make each of us uncomfortable at times—but I don't mind doing that. I have been blessed with a high calling, and I understand that for the one who receives much, much is expected.

Being a vision caster means looking farther down the road and seeing what others have not seen. Such is the case with Nations Ford today. In early 1996, I saw God's hand moving us to expand our facilities and to enlarge our tent. Today, Nations Ford has two locations with over twenty-eight acres, a 1000-seat worship center, a fully-licensed day care center, a family life center, an administrative building, and several education buildings—a total property value in excess of $5 million. These tools of ministry are simply God's provision for the fulfillment of the vision. What is most important is that God's vision for Nations Ford is not complete; it is a work in process. Ours is a vision for the next millenium and it is our firm belief that the best is yet to come!

END NOTES

Introduction

[1] Alvin Toffler, *Future Shock*. (New York: Bantam Books, 1970).

[2] Dale Galloway, *20/20 Vision*. (Portland, Oregon: Scott Publishing Co., 1990).

[3] Stephen Covey, *Principle-Centered Leadership*. (New York: Simon & Shuster, 1990).

Chapter One

[1] Stephen Covey, *Seven Habits of Highly Effective People*. (New York: Simon & Shuster, 1989).

[2] Peter Wagner, *Strategies for Church Growth*. (Ventura, California: Regal Books, 1971).

[3] Lyle Schaller, *44 Questions for Church Planters*. (Nashville: Abingdon Press, 1991).

[4] James Abrahamson, *Put Your Best Foot Forward*. (Nashville: Abington Press, 1994).

[5] Kennon Callahan, *12 Keys to an Effective Church*. (New York: Harper & Row, 1983).

[6] Schaller, Lyle, *44 Ways to Increase Church Attendance*. (Nashville: Abington Press, 1988).

Chapter Two

[1] Stephen Covey, *Principle-Centered Leadership*. (New York: Simon & Shuster, 1990).

Chapter Three

[1] Leith Anderson, *Dying for Change*. (Minneapolis, Minnesota: Bethany House Publishers, 1990).

[2] Wellins, Byham, and Wilson, *Empowered Teams*. (San Francisco: Jossey-Bass Publishers, 1991).

Chapter Four

[1] Victor Frankl, *Man's Search for Meaning*. (Boston: Beacon Press, 1992).

[2] Peter Drucker, *Managing the Non-Profit Organization*. (New York: Harper Business, 1990).

Chapter Five

[1] Hilgert Haimann, *Supervision: Concepts and Practices of Management*. (Cincinnati: South-West Publishing, 1977).

[2] Lyle Schaller, *44 Questions for Church Planters*. (Nashville: Abington Press, 1991).

[3] Galloway, Dale, *20/20 Vision*. (Portland, Oregon: Scott Publishing Co., 1986).

[4] Stephen Covey, *Principle-Centered Leadership*. (New York: Simon & Shuster, 1990).

[5] Oliver Wendall Holmes, taken from *Seven Habits of Highly Effective People Training Manual* by Steven Covey. (Provo, Utah: Covey Leadership Center, 1995.)

Chapter Seven

[1] Leith Anderson, *Dying for Change*. (Minneapolis, Minnesota: Bethany House Publishers, 1990).

[2] Alvin Toffler, *Future Shock*. (New York: Bantam Books, 1970).

[3] Glasser, Sarri, Vinter, *Individual Change Through Small Groups*. (New York: The Free Press, 1974).

[4] J. Sidlow Baxter, *Explore the Book*. (Grand Rapids, Michigan: Zondervan Publishing House, 1960).

[5] Dr. Win Arn, *The Pastor's Church Growth Handbook #1*. (Pasedena, California, 1979).

[6] J. Sidlow Baxter, *Explore the Book*. (Grand Rapids, Michigan: Zondervan Publishing House, 1960).

Chapter Eight

[1] Lyle Schaller, *44 Ways to Increase Church Attendance*. (Nashville: Abington Press, 1988).

[2] Dale Galloway, *Ministry Advantage*, "Twelve Choices For Your Small Group Ministry". (Pasedena, California: Fuller Evangelistic Institute, 1992).

[3] Leith Anderson, *Dying for Change*. (Minneapolis, Minnesota: Bethany House Publishers, 1990).

[4] Wellins, Byham, Wilson, *Empowered Teams*. (San Francisco: Jossey-Bass Publishers, 1991).

[5] Stephen Covey, *Seven Habits of Highly Effective People*. (New York: Simon & Shuster, 1989).

Chapter Nine

[1] Gregory Reed, *Economic Empowerment Through the Church.* (Grand Rapids, Michigan: Zondervan, 1994).

[2] Reed

[3] John Naisbitt, *Megatrends.* (New York: Warner Books, 1984).

[4] Stephen Covey, *Seven Habits of Highly Effective People Training Manual.* (Provo, Utah: Covey Leadership Center, 1995).

www.ingramcontent.com/pod-product-compliance
Lightning Source LLC
Chambersburg PA
CBHW022304060426
42446CB00007BA/585